Bats in the Pavilion

Bats in the Pavilion

A Follow-on from Cricket Mad

Michael Parkinson

Drawings by Derek Alder

Stanley Paul, London

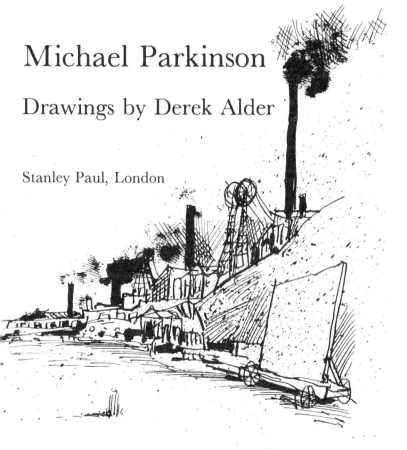

Other books by Michael Parkinson

Cricket Mad
Football Daft
Sporting Fever
Best: An Intimate Biography

Stanley Paul & Co Ltd
3 Fitzroy Square, London W1P 6JD

An imprint of the Hutchinson Publishing Group

London Melbourne Sydney Auckland
Wellington Johannesburg and agencies
throughout the world

First published 1977

**Printed and bound in Great Britain by
Sir Joseph Causton & Sons, Ltd.,
London and Eastleigh.**

ISBN 0 09 131750 9

Contents

Some parts of this book have been developed from articles which I originally wrote for *The Sunday Times* and *Punch*, and I am grateful to the editors of both for allowing me to call on this material.

1 The Game

When it comes to sport I confess to being something like a lady of easy virtue. I have tried everything but enjoyed only a bit of what I sampled. Apart from the obvious sports, I have tangled with the shin-kicking champion of Barnsley and District, played nipsy in the Negev with a lad called Hymie Bracegirdle, and have pimpled to my heart's content in the frozen wastes of Lapland.

Pimpling, in case you didn't know, is a Scandinavian sport whereby you cut a hole in a frozen lake, dangle a line into the water below and hope to catch a fish. Any similarity between this and angling is purely superficial, as the pimpler operates from a prone position lying flat on the ice. Only a reindeer skin is between him and a severe and embarrassing case of frostbite.

It is this unique experience of every kind of sport that puts me in a position to adjudicate on the question of which game requires the greatest range of skills and makes the most rigid demands on mind and body. With hesitation that sport is cricket.

I will not even bother to elaborate my theory that soccer is a simple-minded game for simple-minded people, that golf is merely an expensive way of leaving home, and that the only justification for rugby is that it keeps the participants off the streets for a few hours each week. Suffice it to say cricket is the noblest of games, and I shall tell you why.

To start with, in common with almost every other game, you don't have to be bright to be involved with cricket. The Marylebone Cricket Club has proved that for a century or more. The difference is that to *play* cricket well it actually helps if you have an extra drop of oil in your lamp.

In cricket, more than in any other game, experience and intelligence can triumph over stamina and callow youth.

Cricket is one of the few team games where the forty-year-old can play in the first team without feeling like a pensioner in a nursery school. Indeed, there is evidence to suggest that batsmen and spin bowlers are better in their thirties and forties than they are in the days of their supposed prime.

Tom Graveney only got better as he grew old and Fred Titmus in his autumn years was a connoisseur's joy. Fast bowlers are the exception to the rule, except that Fred Trueman could have survived a few more seasons had he been anything other than a fast bowler in mind as well as body.

Cricket is the most complicated of games to play, the most demanding of mind and spirit and in consequence the most satisfying when played well. Compared to all other games, cricket is chess as against snakes and ladders.

It has one further virtue. It is the most beautiful of games and sometimes is given the most beautiful of settings. I remember well when I was in the army doing my national service, playing a lot of cricket around those lovely counties of Wiltshire and Somerset.

One day we played a Wiltshire village team with a name like Middle Sonning which fitted it like a thatched roof. The ground was concealed in a fold in the hills, flanked on one side by pasture and grazing cows, and on the other by the village with cottages, the church and the pub. It was almost too much, too theatrically beautiful to be true. The day itself was perfect, high summer with birdsong and the smell of woodsmoke and cut grass.

We batted last and when I went to the wicket is was early

'Cricket is chess . . .'

evening and the sun was going down and shadows were spilling on to the pitch. The church bell chimed, the cows chomped the grass, and as I walked to the middle I remember thinking I had died and gone to heaven.

I took guard from a local verger who was umpiring and prepared to take first ball from a left-arm spin bowler who was asking to be walloped. I didn't want to spoil my evening so I decided to play myself in quietly. The first ball was a foot outside the leg stump, but I resisted temptation and padded it to square leg.

'How's that?' said the bowler.

'That's out,' said the umpire.

I looked at him incredulously.

'In this kind of cricket anyway,' he said defiantly.

I left wanting to put that idyllic setting to the torch. That is the real and unique joy of cricket: a magnificent mistress and a terrible bitch.

2 Like Father, Like Son

Maidenhead and Bray Extras XI – which is a polite way of describing the third team – was at one time in danger of being overrun by Parkinsons. There were two of us in the team - myself and Andrew, the fourteen-year old - with two others, Nicholas (ten) and Michael (six), operating the scoreboard.

Moreover, Mrs Parkinson was often the sole spectator, and what is more John William Parkinson, my old man and chieftain of the tribe, was constantly threatening a comeback as an umpire. If this had happened, my old man would've made an umpire with a unique outlook on the job.

For instance, he was the only umpire I knew who constantly offered advice to the bowlers. Thus every delivery was followed by a 'Pitch 'em up' or 'Blow him a bouncer' or 'Get thi' bloody hair cut'. Also, he was one of the few umpires of my experience who appealed along with the bowler. Many's the time he leapt in the air and joined with the bowler in an ear-shattering appeal for lbw, leaving the departing batsman with serious doubts about the supposed impartiality of the adjudicator.

Once he appealed for a catch behind the wicket and discovered to his chagrin, after his cry had echoed round the field, that his had been the only voice raised in anguish. As the fielders and a startled batsman regarded him with

awe, he straightened his tie, cleared his throat and said, 'Not out, you silly old bugger.'

Maidenhead and Bray Extras XI, however, was spared the experience of having my old man as umpire. He delayed his comeback until the party to tour Australia was announced. He lived in hope that they would send for him as baggage man or the like, or that they would consult him in matters of team selection.

He had his team selected for some time. It was: D. B. Close (Somerset), capt. R. Illingworth (Leicestershire), vice-capt. G. Boycott (Yorks), deputy vice-capt., B. Wood (Lancashire), J. Balderstone (Leicestershire), J. H. Wardle (Cambridgeshire), J. Laker (BBC TV Centre), F. S. Trueman (Batley Variety Club), plus the rest of the current Yorkshire side. He feels certain that this team would conquer the world.

However, all that is by the by and nothing whatsoever to do with the Maidenhead and Bray third team, except for the fact that, by playing in the same team as my son, I am reliving the time a million summers ago when I played in the same team with my old man.

In those days he was coming to the end of a career as a fast bowler of real pace and hostility, during which time he had achieved a reputation which made him as welcome on the playing fields of South Yorkshire as a family of moles. He captained the second team and collected around him a gang of raggy-arsed miners' sons which he turned into a cricket team – and a good one at that.

Under his critical gaze we learned the basics of the loveliest of games like play back, play forward and never hook or cut until the crysanthemums have flowered. He taught us the game's intricacies and mysteries, like lifting the seam on the ball with a thumbnail, maintaining its shine with Brylcreem, and the tactical virtue of the bouncer followed by the yorker. 'One to make his eyes water, the other to knock his pegs over,' he'd say.

He was a stickler for doing things properly, for people looking the part. He would not allow anyone in his team who was what he considered to be 'improperly dressed', which in his eyes would be someone wearing black socks or brown plimsolls. At this time there were a good number of youths in our team who didn't own the proper equipment – their parents either didn't care or couldn't afford it – but no one ever took the field in father's team unless he looked like a proper cricketer. He insisted on all of us going to the wicket correctly padded and protected. In those days it was commonplace to see a cricketer wearing one pad and no batting gloves, and a protector was something only wicket-keepers and pansies wore. Father would have none of it and would even admonish youngsters on opposing teams who came to the wicket less than adequately protected.

If the youngster wearing one pad refused his advice to return to the pavilion and put the other pad on, he would take the ball and aim at the unprotected leg. He was still accurate enough to hit it more or less at will and quick enough to make his victim wish he had taken his advice.

Eventually we grew up under his wing and became a team of young men. Then we broke up and went our different ways, some into the first team, some to different clubs and higher leagues. I went to Barnsley and the old man retired to come and watch me play, standing behind the bowler's arm wincing at my foolishness in cutting when the crysanthemums were a long way from flowering.

I used to laugh with him and at him a lot, marking him down as a character and thinking he represented a generation and a life style that was totally different to mine. He was, I reckoned, a man I'd never be.

Then in the past few weeks playing with my son I had the feeling that I was seeing a familiar landscape, the sense that I had been there before. When Andrew threw the new ball to the bowler on the bounce I said, 'Up, up, keep the bloody thing up,' and my father's voice came echoing down the years.

When he made a brilliant stop I grinned like an idiot and when he let the ball through his legs I felt like hitting him with the stump. In one game he had to go out and block for a couple of overs to save the game, and I told him how to play the off spinner with bat and pad together, bat angled down and straight down the line.

I took up my position by the sightscreen playing every ball with him and damn me if he didn't walk down the track to the first ball and drive it through mid-on. It was not what I had told him to do, and I semaphored my displeasure. As I did so I saw the stumper looking at me in an odd way and having a word with my son.

My mind went back more than twenty years when stumpers used to question me about the antics of a middle-aged man leaping about near the sightscreen. 'Who's he, the bloody village idiot?' one of them said to me. 'No, it's my old man,' I said. 'I'm reet sorry for thee, kid,' he said.

So I knew what the wicket-keeper was saying to my son because although the times have changed and everyone in our team wears proper pads and protectors and no one plays in brown plimsolls, the fundamentals remain the same.

The fact is me and my old man are peas from the same pod, like father like son, and what I learned at his knee about the most beautiful of games is part of a heritage that I am now passing on to my sons.

I stood by that sightscreen and didn't care what the stumper was thinking. In that precious moment I was a man contented and fulfilled.

3 Unsung Heroes

When I was very young and dreaming of being Len Hutton
– that was in the days when England had a cricket team – a
cricket pitch was any strip of land approximately twenty-
two yards long. The first floodlit cricket match ever played
was between my Invitation XI and Gonk Reynolds' team
under a street lamp in a Yorkshire mining village near on
thirty years ago. Wisden does not record the fact, but at
that time we didn't know who he was either.

In those earliest formative years the art of batmanship
was a simple matter of protecting your person rather than
defending the wicket. The present crop of England cricketers who play Lillee and Thomson from square leg remind
me irresistibly of my old team who knew that to follow the
classic dictum of getting the nose over the ball simply
meant a two-ounce missile up the left nostril.

Our best pitch was a strip of brown earth near the top
boozer. We ironed out the lumps by jumping on them and
flattened it into submission with the back of a coal shovel.
In the end it resembled the colour and texture of treacle
toffee, but at least it drew the teeth of our budding fast
bowlers who either learned to pitch it up or, alternatively,
joined the card school which rivalled drinking as the
favourite pastime in our village.

Equipment was a problem. We had two bats, one made
from a railway sleeper which must have weighed ten

pounds and was like batting with a sledgehammer, and the other an aged Patsy Hendren autograph bat which had half the blade sawn off so that we kids could handle it. Balls were 'corkies', which had the killing power of cannon balls, sometimes supplemented by wooden balls which we nicked from the coconut shies of the travelling fairs.

In order to raise funds for new equipment we used to lie in wait for the punters from the top boozer. At chucking-out time you could always reckon on a crowd of them lurching across our pitch.

We used to say: 'Bet tha' can't bowl me out mister.' The punter, awash in Barnsley Bitter, would always rise to the challenge. 'How much kid?' he'd say. 'I'll bet thee a tanner tha' can't get me out in twenty balls,' we'd say.

They used to take their coats off, measure out their runs and come charging in like fighting bulls. What happened as they approached the delivery crease always depended on how much they had supped. Some expired in the final stride, some got lost on the way, often ending up facing the establishment they had just left and bowling at the tap-room door.

The few that managed to propel the ball in the general direction of the snotty-nosed kid with the railway sleeper in his hand were soon discouraged by the pitch which suffocated the ball's venom and smothered the bowler's ambition. They'd pay up and go home muttering. On a good day we'd end up with the couple of bob apiece. They didn't know it then but they were, in fact, cricket's first sponsors. Again Wisden didn't record the fact, but, then again, I'll bet he didn't spend much time in the snug at our local boozer.

As far as wickets were concerned, things didn't get better when I joined my first club. The wicket was what could be politely termed 'sporting'.

It wasn't the fault of the groundsman, a lovely crotchety old soul called Cheyney. He tried hard, but there was too much wrong with the square ever to get it right.

Cheyney was a great believer in using animal droppings as fertilizer, and he always used to carry a bucket with him whenever he went about the village in case some horse along the way might oblige him with a dollop of dressing for his pitch. We had the dubious distinction of not only having one of the worst pitches in the world, but also the smelliest. At the same time you could argue that we had the cleanest streets in Britain because Cheyney's pursuit of horse droppings was tireless and meticulous.

He was once invited along to the local evening class to give a lecture on the art of being a groundsman. Being a man of few words, he didn't waste any. 'The secret of making grass grow is 'oss muck', he said, and sat down. The audience who expected a somewhat lengthier dissertation stirred uncomfortably. The chairman asked nervously: 'Surely there must be something else?' Cheyney shook his head: 'Nowt but more 'oss muck,' he replied.

Some time later, after old Cheyney was dead and buried, they built a super new sports stadium on the site of his wicket. They dedicated it to Dorothy Hyman, who was born in the village. I opened it amid much splendour and civic pomp, but nobody mentioned that it was built on a ton of Cheyney's horse manure.

It wasn't until I went to the local grammar school that I discovered the joy of batting on a proper wicket. The pitch was carved from a hillside high above Barnsley. It was an unlikely setting for a treasure, but there is no doubt in my mind that the wicket I played on for the next five seasons was the best batting track I have ever encountered. It was fast and true and in good weather possessed that lovely sheen which meant runs for anyone who could play straight and an afternoon of purgatory for any bowler who strayed from all but the strictest line and length.

About that time I had given up being Len Hutton in order to emulate my great hero, Keith Miller, but I quickly gave up all ambitions of being an all-rounder after my first bowl on that wicket. I went back to Len. Stouter hearts than mine tried to hammer some life out of it, but none succeeded. These bowlers were not only discouraged by the absolute perfection of the strip, but also by the attitude of the groundsman, John Matthewman.

He was a taciturn man, only moved to displays of emotion when fast bowlers with large feet ploughed up his precious turf. Then he would spend the game pacing the boundary muttering about the vandals who were trampling on his work of art. We once played against a team with a fast bowler who dragged his back foot alarmingly. Moreover, he possessed a pair of boots reinforced with steel plates which gave them the appearance of a pair of ironclads and did to our pitch what the invading Goths did to ancient Rome.

At the end of our innings the groundsman was beside himself with rage. He invited the offending bowler to inspect the damage he had caused. Together they stared at the scarred turf.

'Just look what tha's done,' said John, in sorrow and anger.

'Well, it's mi drag tha' sees,' said the bowler.

'Drag?' said John.

'Tha' sees I drag mi toe when I'm bowling,' the bowler explained.

'Whoever bowled on his sodding toes. Whoever heard of such a thing,' said John. 'Anyway what's them?' he asked, indicating the player's boots.

'Reinforced toe-caps,' the bowler said.

'Reinforced toe-caps. I've nivver heard of anything so daft. They look like bloody pit boots. Bowling on his toes with pit boots on. A bloody ballet dancer wearing pit boots. Whoever heard of such a thing,' said John, by now on his knees trying to repair the damage.

If the idiosyncrasies of fast bowlers were a complete and utter mystery to him there wasn't a single thing he didn't know about the preparation of a cricket pitch. Before we were allowed to set foot on one of his masterpieces he inspected it inch by inch armed with a cut-throat razor, trimming a blade of grass that dared to be a millimetre out of uniform length, slitting the throat of any weed that had the audacity to believe it might flourish while he was around. When he had finished he would give us the nod.

'What's it like?' we'd say, as part of the ritual.

'If tha' can play cricket tha'll get runs,' was what he'd always reply. And he was as good as his word.

When I left that school I moved down the hill to Barnsley Cricket Club and, shortly after, John Matthewman came down, too. Ask any knowledgeable cricketer to name the best batting tracks in Yorkshire and John Matthewman's Barnsley wicket is sure to be mentioned.

Whenever I think back on the game I love most of all I remember that slab of earth in a Yorkshire pit village where I first played the game and then of John Matthewman's two masterpieces where I learned to play the game properly. I calculate the difference and in doing so assess what I and hundreds of other players owe to John Matthewman and people like him.

I thought of him a lot when I heard he had died. A local death not warranting a mention in the national press. A groundsman dies, a man whose simple job it was to shape earth, grass, wind, rain and sun into a cricket pitch. On the face of it that is all there is to it. Yet I know he was an artist, and so do many others who were acquainted with his work. Often he achieved perfection, and how many of us will go to the grave able to say that one, ultimately fulfilling, thing?

4 How to Pick a Team
PART 1

Once upon a time there were five dwarfs, and they lived in great style at the Marylebone Clodpoles Club. They were called Dopey, Dizzy, Dozy, Drippy and Gormless. One day they were visited by their small nephew, who had been sent to stay with them while his parents attended a wife-swapping convention in Rotherham.

When he arrived the small boy came upon a curious scene. One dwarf was picking names from a hat, another was reading tea leaves and two others were boiling toads' eyes and bats' wings in a heavy cauldron and chanting in monotonous voices while rattling bones over the putrid brew. There was no sign of the fifth dwarf.

'What are you doing?' asked the small boy.

'Picking the England cricket team,' said Dopey.

'How very curious,' said the small boy.

'Not curious at all,' said Dizzy and Drippy in unison, looking up from their steaming cauldron.

'Very scientific, in fact,' said Dozy, stirring the tea leaves.

'It seems silly to me,' said the small boy. 'I mean, surely picking a cricket team is like anything else. You simply pick the best players.'

A ghastly silence fell upon the room. The only sound to be heard was from the hubble-bubble of the cauldron.

Finally, Dopey, who seemed to be the chief dwarf, spoke

up. 'It is not that easy, young man. You are not just picking any old team when you pick the England cricket team. It is a very specialized business. First, we put the names in the hat, and then we pull them out one by one. That is my job. As I read out the names we inspect the tea leaves to see if the signs are propitious. Finally, we drop all the names into yonder putrid brew, and if it turns red, white and blue we have a side.'

'Do the Australians pick their cricket team the same way?' asked the small boy.

Again a ghastly silence fell upon the room. Finally, Dopey spoke again, this time in a strained voice.

'Our cousins in the Antipodes have a lot to learn about selecting a cricket team,' he said.

'But they thrash us regularly, so they must do a better job than you,' said the small boy.

'What has losing got to do with it?' said Dopey. 'We have never been guilty of picking a side just to beat the opposition. That is a crude and common approach. We are picking emissaries of our fair and sceptred isle to bring culture and learning to inferior tribes in the remotest corners of the earth.'

'I see,' said the small boy. 'But do the other teams realize that is what you do?'

'They have been getting the message of late,' said Dopey, somewhat ruefully.

The small boy was getting tired of the conversation which he thought was very silly and, furthermore, the smell of the putrid brew had given him a headache.

'Where is Uncle Gormless?' he asked.

'Ah, he is locked away doing the most important job of all,' said Dopey.

'What is that?' asked the small boy.

'Selecting the new England captain,' he said.

'I'd like to see that,' said the small boy.

His Uncle Dopey, who was a kind man really, looked at him patiently, smiled, and said: 'You do know that the selection of the England cricket captain is one of life's great mysteries, like the function of the human appendix or the medicinal properties of young rhubarb. It is a secret handed down from generation to generation and known only to a handful of members of the Marylebone Clodpoles Club.'

'How very curious,' said the young boy.

'There are some things that should only be known to a few,' said Dopey, sagely. 'However, I will give you a rare treat. I will take you to your Uncle Gormless so that you might be initiated into one of life's more profound ceremonies.' .

He led the young boy from the room and up several flights of stairs until they came upon a beautiful ivory tower. Sitting in the middle of the room in the lotus position, naked except for an MCC tie and a Free Foresters cap, was Uncle Gormless. He was surrounded by books.

'How are your parents?' he asked the small boy.

'Very well, sir. They are attending a wife-swapping convention in Rotherham,' he said.

'What is wife-swapping?' asked Uncle Gormless.

'A new sport sweeping the nation, or so I believe,' said Uncle Dopey, who secretly read the *News of the World* on the toilet.

'My dad says it's more fun than cricket,' said the little boy.

'How little they know,' said Uncle Gormless, patting the small boy's head in a patronizing fashion.

'How long have you been doing this job?' asked the small boy.

'One hundred and three years come next Michaelmas,' said Uncle Gormless.

'Without stopping?' asked the small boy.

'I haven't been well in recent years, and one or two outsiders like Hutton, Close and that Illingworth fella got in while I was away. But now I am back in command and things are as they should be,' he said.

'How do you go about your job?' asked the small boy.

'I am about to impart a secret known to few mortals,' said Gormless. 'Firstly, I use my books of reference. *Debrett, Burke's Peerage,* the *Army List, Crockford's Clerical Directory* and bound back issues of the Eton College magazine. Working through these volumes I light upon a suitable name, check the fella's antecedents, and if he seems a decent enough chap then we give him the job.'

'But supposing he can't play cricket?' asked the small boy.

'Ah, but that is the point. It doesn't matter. In your innocence you have stumbled on the secret of my job. You won't tell a soul will you?' said Uncle Gormless.

'But my dad knows your secret. He says it's obvious that the one qualification needed by an England captain is that he mustn't be good enough to get in the side,' said the small boy.

Uncle Gormless was deeply shocked by the news. His body went rigid; his patriarchial face under the Free Foresters cap was deeply troubled. He closed his eyes and began frothing at the mouth.

'Is anything wrong?' asked the small boy.

'He's talking to Lord Hawke. He always does that when he has a problem,' said Uncle Dopey.

He led the small boy from the room. As he left the boy lingered for a moment and watched the gibbering figure sitting cross-legged on the floor surrounded by books. His Uncle Dopey took him downstairs to the front door. He gave him 10p and said: 'Go and feed the monkeys at the zoo. You have seen enough for one day.'

The small boy trudged away from the Marylebone Clodpoles Club towards London Zoo. He wasn't upset. His dad had told him that they all wanted their heads testing.

As he walked along, his mind full of strange imaginings, wondering, for instance, if his Uncle Gormless might give him the chance of captaining England, lots of things were happening in the world around him.

They were building Disneyland at Lord's, Headingley was a bingo hall and the Oval had just been declared a disaster area. In the meantime, our distant cousins in the far-flung corners of the world were licking their lips at the prospect of the coming world cricket competition, like predators sensing an easy kill.

In an ivory tower in London the future of English cricket was being decided. 'But supposin' W.G. doesn't want the job?' Uncle Gormless was asking Lord Hawke.

5 How to Pick a Team
PART 2

The mysterious fire which destroyed Lord's last week is believed to have started in the committee room. There is still no news of the England selectors who were using the room at the time. Police are puzzled by their disappearance, but say they have no reason to suspect foul play.

It was shortly before midnight on Friday when a passer-by heard an explosion and saw flames billowing out of the pavilion. Police and firemen were quickly on the scene, but were unable to prevent the building being gutted.

Eye witnesses report hearing strange noises in the pavilion shortly before the explosion. One man described 'wailing and moaning' coming from the direction of the committee room, followed by 'bitter sobbing'. Then, he said, he heard what sounded like pistol shots followed by a large explosion which caused the blaze. Police have ruled out the possibility of a lover's tiff or a suicide pact.

Also missing in the blaze are G. O. Allen and F. R. Brown, who are believed to have been in the committee room at the time. Although not on the selection panel, both men have earned deserved reputations for the guidance they have given the selectors throughout the years. They are believed to have chosen the majority of the England captains since the war, and therefore must take great credit for the present state of English cricket.

Police say that other fatalities in the tragedy were M C C

members who were asleep in the Long Room at the time. They were (in order or rank): Rear Admiral Egbert Dripping, Brigadier R. Varicose-Arbuthnot, Mr Justice Shagnasty and the Bishop of Basutoland. Inquests on six other bodies recovered from the Long Room were adjourned after medical evidence revealed they had been dead for several years.

Tony Grovel, England's South African captain, appeared on BBC television and, with the aid of sub-titlès, paid moving tribute to the England selectors. He said they would be sadly missed, particularly by the cricketers of other countries, who held them in great regard. Mr Grovel said that wherever he went in the world he never heard the opposition say a bad word about our selectors.

Looking to the future, Mr Grovel said we should not get despondent. Selection of the England team in future would be made by Mr E. W. Swanton and his old colleagues on the *Daily Telegraph*. Mr Grovel pointed out that this new departure was not as novel as it at first seemed if you took into account the fact that Mr Swanton had been picking the England team for years.

Mr Grovel said he was not downhearted about England's dismal showing in recent years. He said we should look at the bright side of things. For instance, until the Old Trafford Test, England had not lost a game under his captaincy. We hadn't won one either, but that was neither here nor there.

Referring to the defeat at Old Trafford, Mr Grovel said that when you looked at it objectively the only difference between the two sides was Greenidge, Fredericks, Richards, Kallicharran, Lloyd, Roberts, Holding and Daniel – otherwise it could well have been a very different story. What is more, England had not been helped by the weather. Normally rain severely affected play at Old Trafford, and the selectors always took this into consideration when choosing the team to play there.

Elaborating on this statement, Mr Grovel said that traditionally selection for the Manchester Test was always made bearing in mind the long, boring hours spent in the pavilion watching the rain come down. Therefore a player was selected as much for his social talent as his playing skill.

Thus Mike Selvey was chosen because of his fine harmonica playing, and Frank Hayes for his remarkable impersonation of George Formby. Mike Hendrick would never have been picked if the selectors had thought it was going to be a proper cricket match, and only got his place on this occasion because of his virtuosity on the nose-flute.

Mr Grovel said the public should bear all this in mind before bashing the players and the selectors. As for his own form, Mr Grovel said he was far from satisfied but not downhearted. Moreover, he felt his accordion playing and spirited rendition of Afrikaans folk songs gave him the edge over any contenders.

Asked to predict the outcome of next season's series against Australia, Mr Grovel said he intended to 'greig'* them.

A momentous day for English cricket was climaxed when Mr E. W. Swanton, the new chairman of selectors, announced the England side for the final Test. It is: A. W. Grovel (Sussex capt.), Michael Melford (*Daily Telegraph*), Tony Lewis (*Sunday Telegraph*), Lord Longford (Holloway CC), Duke of Alburquerque (Neasden CC), Sir Campbell Adamson (CBICC), Peter West (Victor Silvester CC), Sir Harold Wilson (Batley Variety Club), Nawab of Pataudi (Southall CC), Lord Porchester (Jockey Club) and Lionel Blair. Lord Lucan is twelfth man.

---

* 'To greig', pronounced 'grigg'. An Afrikaans word meaning to be fallen on from a great height.

6 How to Run the Game

As soon as his team were beaten by an innings and 152 runs by neighbouring Muscat and Oman, the prince, never a man to let the oil gush beneath his feet, was on the blower to me.

'El Parky, the Wise One?' he asked.

'The very same,' I retorted, quick as a flash.

'I want you to reorganize the game of cricket in my country. I want administrators, players and coaches. You have twenty-five million pounds to spend in five years, by which time I expect my team to win the Prudential Trophy,' he said.

'First, your highness, you must buy Lord's,' I said.

'Lord's? What is that?' he said.

'It is the fountainhead of all cricket, and its occupants are much attuned to your way of life in that they discourage women from the inner sanctums, and forbid any unseemly displays of the human body, be it male or female, on the premises.

'Many of its members are known to be in favour of your ancient punishments of castration, beheading and disembowelling of offenders and would, therefore, integrate perfectly in your society,' I said.

'This is unbelievable,' said the prince.

'There is one snag,' I said.

'Tell me.'

'These people, so admirable and suitable in many respects, consume great quantities of gin and tonic,' I said.

'Alcohol is forbidden by our Koranic law,' he said.

'They won't come without it,' I said.

'Nobody's perfect,' he said with a sigh.

'Your highness displays all the wisdom of his illustrious forebearers,' I said.

'Now what about the administration?' he asked.

'We have the finest in the world. Men who are responsible for English cricket being where it is today,' I said proudly.

'What qualifications do they have?' he asked.

'Your highness,' I said, my voice taking on the slightly condescending tone I use when addressing children, idiots and foreigners, 'what you must realize about cricket is that unlike other games, it does not believe in hiring administrators who are qualified to do the job. That is professionalism of the worst kind.

'We much prefer the tried and trusted principles of pedigree. For instance, if a man went to public school, got a blue at university and learned how to play with a straight bat, we consider he has all the attributes necessary to run our game of cricket.'

'I see. Can they be bought?' he asked.

'If you purchase Lord's you get them for nothing. They go with the building,' I explained.

'Superb! Now what about teaching us how to play the game properly?'

'First of all, I must know about your pitches,' I said.

'Well, we play on baked sand mixed with a little oil,' he said.

'Splendid. There is a firm in London specializing in that technique. I shall contact Mr George Davis immediately. The trick is to prepare wickets that give no assistance whatsoever to either spin bowlers or bowlers of extreme pace.

'This brings everyone down to your level and, moreover,

guarantees Test matches lasting five days. Next we shall send our Test batsman over to coach your players in the techniques of the forward defensive push and the backward defensive jab. This will guarantee that your players will eventually be able to bat for five days if they so desire. They won't score any runs, but neither will they get out.

'Then we will show your bowlers how to bowl short of a length to defensive fields, making it difficult for the other side to score runs. Finally, and this is most important, we shall demonstrate how to slow the game down to thirteen or fourteen overs an hour, making it impossible for the other side to win.'

There was silence at the other end of the line. I was about to tell him to put another oil well in the slot when he said, 'El Parky, the Wise One?'

'The very same,' I said.

'I came to you to seek wisdom, to learn from the lips of the people who invented cricket how best my country might win the Prudential Trophy,' he said. 'From what you have told me you will drive even my countrymen to drink.'

'That is why they sup all that gin and tonic at Lord's,' I explained.

'Truly, is this the way you play cricket in England?' he asked.

'Truly,' I replied.

'With what result?'

'We manage to keep our heads above water,' I said gaily.

'But do you win many games?'

'Not a lot,' I replied.

'But I want my country to win a Test match,' he said.

'Then you've come to the wrong place, your highness,' I said.

'Any suggestions?' he asked.

'Do you know someone called Ian Chappell?' I replied.

7 Tales Worth Telling

At the very beginning of *Close of Play*, by Neville Cardus, there is a cartoon by that talented man, Bernard Hollo-wood. It shows two boys standing before a wall with stumps chalked on it. One is a ragamuffin, the other bespectacled and bookish. The latter is saying to the rapscallion, 'No, you be Len Hutton. I'll be Neville Cardus.'

Although my eyesight is perfect, and not even my best friend could describe me as widely read, I have always associated myself with the bookworm in the cartoon. I wouldn't have minded being Len Hutton, but I would have sold my soul to have been blessed with Sir Neville's gifts.

I still find it difficult to believe his confession that most of those marvellous quotes he attributes to the cricketers he wrote about were invented. And yet I was prepared to do so, because I heard the same statement from his own lips the one and only time I met him.

We lunched together, and because at the time I was gathering material for an article about Wilfred Rhodes, I asked him the source of one of my favourite anecdotes about Wilfred which Sir Neville had written. The story concerns Charles McGahey, the old Essex player, going out to bat on a sunny day at Bramall Lane, Sheffield. As he walked out to face Rhodes the weather changed. Looking over his shoulder at the darkening sun and anticipating a sticky wicket, McGahey said 'Ullo! McGahey caught Tunnicliffe bowled Rhodes...O.' And so it was, both innings.

Sir Neville smiled at the memory and then said, disarmingly, 'Oh, I made it up.' It was my first traumatic experience. He went on to explain that his job was to write scripts for the cricketers who, in the main, were unable to say what they undoubtedly would have said had they possessed Sir Neville's imagination. As he expounded his theory, he must have seen the look of disappointment on my face.

'You mustn't worry, young man, because it happens to be true,' he said.

'What was true?' I asked, somewhat baffled.

'McGahey caught Tunnicliffe bowled Rhodes both innings,' said Sir Neville, as if that explained everything.

Sir Neville's confession raises the whole question of the validity of the sporting anecdote. I once asked Fred Trueman, who has been the subject of more stories than any cricketer in the history of the game, how many were true. 'About ten per cent,' he said.

He didn't mind the majority of them – indeed, he was flattered – but there were one or two he could do without. The story he really objected to, and has spent a lifetime trying to deny, was the one about him sitting next to a high dignitary of the Indian Government at dinner, digging him in the ribs and saying: 'Ayup Gunga Din, pass t'salt.'

All that Fred's denials have achieved is another punchline to the story whereby the teller states that when asked about the yarn's validity, Fred said: 'It's a lie. I never said that. It were t'chutney I were after.'

Although that particular story was an original in that it was invented especially for Fred, quite a few of the others he inherited from the folk-lore of fast bowlers. The one about Fred objecting to a 'fancy hat' cocking a toe at him and, after sufficient warning, dropping a 90 mph yorker on the offending article, was told about Kortright, as well as Larwood, before Fred inherited it.

In the Kortright version the bowler is alleged to have told the batsman that he allowed only one batsman to lift his toe at him, and that was W. G. Grace. The batsman declined the advice and was carried from the field.

In the Larwood—Trueman version, the stricken batsman falls to the floor in anguish. Fieldsmen gather round and remove pad, sock and boot and solicitously massage the bruised foot. After much palaver, the batsman is able to replace his gear and stand up. As he picks up his bat and prepares to continue, Harold/Fred, who has been watching the performance says:

'Are tha' alreet young feller?'

'Yes, thank you very much,' says the batsman.

'Can tha' walk?'

'I think so, thank you.'

'Good. Well, get thissen off to t'pavilion because tha'rt lbw,' says Harold/Fred.

A lovely story, but Fred denies it, and I'll bet it never happened to Larwood nor to Kortright. It doesn't really matter because as Sir Neville always believed, cricketers should concentrate on what they do best and leave the legends to those whose job it is to invent them.

An interesting variation on that story concerns Arthur Wood, wicket-keeper in the great Yorkshire side of the thirties. Yorkshire were playing one of the universities and were having their ambition to get home on the second day slightly thwarted by the elegant defence of some young buck. At the start of an over bowled by the great Hedley Verity, Wood decided to take matters in hand. After every ball he would say to the batsman: 'Well played, young sir', or 'Fine shot, young man', so that by the sixth ball of the over the batsman was so convinced of his own mastery that he advanced down the wicket preparatory to hitting Verity out of sight. As he did so he heard Wood say:

'Tha's missed it young man. Now p--off, we've got a train to catch.'

I asked Fred to tell me a true story about himself, and he recounted a bizarre incident which happened on his one and only tour of India for the Royal Cricket Association's Silver Jubilee matches. According to Fred, he was enduring a long and gruelling journey when the train made a stop at a tiny station a million miles from nowhere. Fred decided to stretch his legs and, wandering on to the platform, met the stationmaster. The official was delighted at meeting the great man, and was overjoyed when Fred asked him where the toilets were.

He insisted on taking Fred into the station buildings and into a room where – and Fred avows this to be true – he drew back a curtain and unveiled a Victorian chamber pot which had F. S. Trueman written on it.

How the railwayman knew that one day F. S. Trueman would step off a train at his station and, moreover, want to use his toilet, is a story beyond the imaginings of a Cardus. How long he had waited, and what gave him the idea, no one knows. What happened to the chamber pot, whether it occupies pride of place in the stationmaster's trophy cabinet, or has become a monument of historical interest for the tourist trade, we shall likely never know.

'Is that a true story, F.S.?' I asked.

'Would I tell you a lie, Parky, my old son?' he said.

I didn't answer. They knighted Sir Neville for his embellishments, and by the same token I reckon that if Fred was having me on, he ought to get the Pulitzer Prize for Literature. Moreover, if it is fiction and it passes into the Trueman mythology, Fred will have the supreme satisfaction of knowing that at least one of the lies told about him was of his own invention.

8 Cricket Widows

Contemplating the meaning of life one day, I fell to wondering why the wife had started bringing me cups of tea in bed and generally attending to my every need. I have lived with her too long to believe that such care and consideration sprang naturally from her sunny nature. In other words, there had to be an angle.

'You seem very happy lately,' I remarked.

'Blissfully,' she said.

'May I ask why?' I asked.

It's because you haven't been able to play cricket this season,' she said.

I should have known. It was the first year since we were married that I hadn't flitted o'er the greensward, a state of affairs brought about by a back injury which seriously reduced my chances of making the Test team before I am fifty.

'You have no idea how marvellous it has been to have you home on Saturdays and Sundays, not to mention all those sweaty shirts, socks and jockstraps I no longer have to wash,' she said.

It was a sad moment for a man who had spent a lifetime perfecting the tightrope existence between devotion to family and dedication to cricket.

But it wasn't until I found the plasticine doll with the needle stuck in the lumbar region that I realized just what lengths a woman will go to prevent her man from nipping off to the cricket club on summer weekends.

Such a traumatic experience set me thinking about women and their relationship to cricket, and my observations may be of some use to fellow cricketers who find themselves torn 'twixt house and hutch.

First of all, it is important for the young unmarried player to take as much care in choosing a wife as he would in selecting a new bat – and I can put it no higher than that. When I used to take girls home, my old man's opening gambit was: 'Do you like cricket? Because if you don't there's not much future here.'

Sadly, it is a certain fact that it is easier to choose a cricket bat than pick a wife. A bat is about feel and balance, it either suits your hands or it doesn't. While it could be argued that much the same rule also applies to women, there is one important difference. A bat has a watermark of quality – the grain. If it be straight and unblemished, the chances are you'll have a friend for life. The one basic flaw in the otherwise perfect construction of women is that you can't detect the knots in the grain until it's too late.

On the whole, women who marry weekend cricketers start off promisingly, helping with the teas, sunbathing on the boundary, sharing a 'half' in the bar. This happy condition lasts only a short time, and the woman quickly assumes the tight-lipped, disapproving countenance of the creature known as a 'cricket widow'.

This species never turns up to watch a game, only arrives at the bar to tell the husband the dog ate his dinner and falls asleep just as you are telling her how you won the match single-handed. The husbands of these harridans are easily discernible because their flannels are never clean, they look as if they have slept in their shirts and their socks are a series of holes held together by the odd strand of wool.

Not all women become cricket widows. Some work on the principle that if you can't beat 'em join 'em and so do sterling work with teapots and cheese and chutney sand-

'The husbands of these harridans are easily discernible.'

wiches and the like. This is how things should be, with women happily labouring while their men disport themselves, and anyone challenging that statement knows nothing about the natural order of things.

The last species of women in cricket are those who actually play the game and, in many ways, I find these the most disturbing of the lot. I do not wish women to stop playing cricket, but I do believe – as I do about their sisters in sport at Wimbledon – that they shouldn't do it in public. Women playing cricket should treat it as a matter between consenting females in private, and this would eliminate the embarrassing comparisons that are made with the game as it is properly played by men.

I know the militant female cricketers will be quick to point out their long history, and the fact that over-arm bowling was invented by women who found it impossible to bowl under-arm because of their voluminous skirts. While acknowledging this not considerable contribution to the development of cricket, I must point out that it becomes insignificant compared to the screw-in stud, the hollowed-out bat, the light-weight protector and the googly – all examples of men's never-ceasing genius for invention and technical change.

Nor would I place much importance on the women cricketers' statement that people will take them more seriously when they have played at Lord's. What they don't realize is that this particular establishment has been full of old women for more than a hundred years, and a few more through the front door won't make the slightest difference.

The real fact is that women and cricket don't mix. At one level the game is enough of a mistress to make any wife jealous, and at another it is too masculine a pastime for any woman to conquer. The only women who are suited to the game are those enthusiasts who keep a love of cricket in true perspective. What I mean to say is that while capable of appreciating a cover-drive, they are equally adept at making a pile of potted meat sandwiches, and never object to their husbands' summertime obsession.

Excuse me while I show the wife what I've written. If I don't come back tell them the plasticine doll is under the mattress on her side of the bed.

9 Kamikaze Cricketers

One of the real delights of the summer of 1975 was to witness two marvellous wicket-keepers parading their skills in such very different ways. The only thing Alan Knott and Rodney Marsh have in common is that they both wear wicket-keeping gloves. To be stumped by Knott is to have your pocket picked, to be dismissed by Marsh is something like being mugged.

The Australian's taking of the quick bowlers, his extraordinary anticipation, the magnificent certainty of his catching and the athleticism, surprising in one so chunky, made him one of the stars of the tour. Knott was what he invariably is, a model of consistency and an indefatigable example to his side.

To watch Knott at work through a long, hot day is to understand the old dictum that when picking a cricket team you first choose the 'keeper and then the rest. At the end of the most exhausting session, he was moving to poor returns from tired fielders and making them look good. His unbroken concentration behind the stumps, and his jaunty stride between them at the over's end, were constant reminders to knackered fielders that the day wasn't through.

I enjoyed watching Marsh and Knotty because wicket-keepers fascinate me. They always have done, ever since the days of my youth when the 'keeper was the lad who stood behind the dustbin and threw his coat at the corky.

When he graduated to the local club side, he inherited the stumper's pads, which were taller and twice as wide as ordinary pads. His protector was an iron cup fastened beneath a corselet to protect his stomach, and the gloves were of leather so stiff and thick that we had to rub them with dubbin to get them to bend. Thus attired, he would stride to the wicket looking like a cross between the Michelin Man and one of those poor padded horses that are used as chopping blocks in Spanish bull-rings.

Often, due to the appalling state of our wickets and the homicidal nature of our fast bowlers, the 'keeper used to add his own personal item of protection. This always depended upon the part of the anatomy most prized by the individual. You could tell a lot about a man from the parts he protected.

The most cautious wicket-keeper we ever had used to wrap a towel round his thighs, protect his chest with a cushion up his jumper and complete the ensemble with a

pair of goggles much favoured by motorcyclists and those defeated German officers we used to see in all the films about how we won the war in the desert. His appearance was further enhanced by an absence of teeth, which he left in a pint pot in the dressing-room, and the presence of steel toe-caps on his boots.

His one vanity was a toupé affixed to his head by a miraculous substance which defied both boiling sun and raging storm to shift it. Moreover, it was impervious to the local air pollution, which was capable of taking the enamel from your teeth and rotting your wellies.

I mention this fact because, had our 'keeper treated his gloves with the marvellous adhesive that held his wig to his scalp, he would have been one of the best in the business. As it was, his one fault was that he was totally incapable of catching the ball. He compensated for his lack of technique by simply letting the ball hit him. He would stand straight as a guardsman and always over the stumps, no matter how quick the bowler, and stop the ball with whichever part of his body it was aimed at. He reminded me irresistibly of one of those sandbags used for bayonet practice on an assault course.

In his favour, it must be said that although he didn't take many catches (indeed the only one he caught lodged in the top of his pads), neither did he let many past him. Moreover, he was the best cheat behind the stumps I ever saw.

He was adept at dislodging the bails with a nudge of his knees, thus claiming numerous wickets from balls that had just cleared the top of stumps. He dispelled any doubts in the umpire's mind by shouting 'Good ball, lad!' and immediately replacing the bail before a doubt had even a chance to harden into an objection. Most of the batsmen knew they had been done, but few were brave enough to argue with the grotesque monster that had diddled them.

From the way I have described him, it would seem that his true place in sporting history would be in the gallery of eccentrics along with people like Evel Knievel and the man who tried to clear the Manchester Ship Canal with a hop, skip and a jump. In fact he is nothing of the sort. He is one of a glorious line of heroes who had braved the most daunting task in all of sport.

If a captain were to issue instructions to a wicket-keeper as to his duties on the field of play they would, I am sure, closely resemble the orders given to kamikaze pilots before setting off on a suicide mission. That players like Knott and Marsh, John Murray and Bob Taylor, Bairstow and Engineer, could turn it into an art form is a triumph against all the odds. That lesser mortals, like my mate with the hairpiece, try it at all is further proof that no matter how much the world changes, there is still one born every minute.

10 My Back Yard

My cricket garden is looking lovely. The Geoffrey Boycott rose is blooming beautifully, the strip of Brammall Lane turf is doing as well as can be expected under an alien sun, and the two willow trees – named Gunn and Moore – weep gently for English cricket.

The numbing tranquility of this perfect setting is only disturbed by the regular appearance of a ginger moggy who has taken a liking to weeing on Geoffrey Boycott. I have nicknamed the intruder Gubby and amuse myself by disturbing his ablutions with a well-directed yorker.

To give you a better idea of this paradise on earth I have to describe the setting as I stride out to take first knock. I come out of the french windows, down the terrace steps and take guard facing the river. The green shed with the broken windows is the wicket, Gunn and Moore are at mid-off and mid-on, while Geoffrey Boycott looks ravishing at deep point. The river is behind the bowler's arm, this being the only cricket pitch in the world where long-on requires a boat or, alternatively, the facility to walk on water. A ball in the river is six and out except if it is caught by the occupant of a passing pleasure cruiser, in which case the game is abandoned while we all race down to the nearest lock to retrieve it.

Visiting batsmen find it difficult to adjust to these unique conditions, but their problems are slight compared

to the bowler's. The wicket is atop a small plateau approached at the bowler's end by a gentle slope which suddenly sprouts into a small mountain. Thus the last few yards of the bowler's run are up an almost vertical face and, if he is not careful, the delivery stride is likely to end with the back foot half way down the mountain and the front foot on the plateau. This is a somewhat inelegant and painful position which has been known to make the bowler's eyes water.

Some players, anticipating the difficulty beforehand, have tried delivery while running up the mountain with the result that the ball is propelled towards the heavens and eventually drops in front of the batsman after a trajectory like a mortar bomb.

No one, except the Parkinsons, has twigged that the only way to bowl on your wicket is to do away with a run-up and deliver from a standing position. Thus it is that all my team – myself and my three sons – constitute the only all-spin attack in the world. Number One son and I bowl off-spin in the manner of the great Illingworth, Number Two son bowls leg breaks and googlies and Number Three son is the secret weapon, the only child lob bowler in the history of first-class cricket.

He has broken many a long stand by his habit of bursting into tears after being thrashed to the boundary. Whenever that happens the rest of the Parkinsons stare at the batsman as if he ought to be ashamed of himself whereupon, more often than not, he surrenders his wicket next ball out of sheer remorse and in order to stop the waterworks.

If this mixture of spin and guile fails to work we have one surprise left. Number One son who, all else apart, is well on the way to becoming the eating champion of the world, has perfected a way of exploiting the natural and unique charms of our pitch to bowl the unplayable ball. I should explain that apart from the mountainous appraoch there is one further hazard to the bowler which is Gunn, the willow tree. Although standing at mid-off, he weeps all over the run-up making a straightforward approach impossible to all, except to Number One son.

When bowling his 'super-ball' he starts his run from the base of the willow thereby being hidden from the batsman whose only warning of impending doom is a rustling in the undergrowth. Still undetected Number One son charges up the mountain and when near the summit leaps upwards and forwards so that he bursts through the overhanging willow folliage and lands on the bowling crease.

The tramatic abruptness of his appearance, heightened by the noise of breaking branches and fleeing birds, is too much for the batsman who, more often than not, is bowled while in a state of acute shock.

As I say, we only use this technique when all else fails because Old Gunn is the subject of a preservation order, and I don't want to be the one up before the Beak who tries to explain that it died of fast bowling.

When my father was alive, I would've been willing to sacrifice the tree in the national interest, which is to say that if England seemed likely to get another drubbing from the Australians I would have been willing to hand over my pitch for a Test match. The condition would be that I should be allowed to pick the England team, in which case is would have read: John William Parkinson (Grimethorpe Colliery and Yorks), capt. Michael Parkinson Snr. (Barnsley and Yorks), Andrew Parkinson (Wakefield Nursing Home and Yorks), Nicholas Parkinson and Michael Parkinson Jr. (c/o Mary Parkinson, former spinster of the parish of Doncaster, Yorks), G. Boycott (Yorks), J. Hampshire (Yorks), D. Bairstow (Yorks), A. G. Nicholson (Yorks).

Just in case I stood accused of being biased in favour of one county I would have completed the side with two-outsiders, namely Close, of Somerset, and Illingworth, of Leicester. And, to prove my true impartiality, Wood of Lancashire would have been my twelfth man.

Given that line-up and my pitch we could have taken on the world and re-established ourselves as champions. We might have had to change the side slightly for overseas tours (my old man would not travel to any place where they didn't serve Yorkshire pudding as a starter), but the immediate priority was to get English cricket back to where it belonged.

I await a visit from Mr Bert Lock, the inspector of pitches. In the meantime you must excuse me because Gubby is interfering with Geoff Boycott yet again.

11 Cricket in the Bud

The future of English cricket was to be seen at Abingdon getting changed in the hedge bottom. Fred hadn't turned up with the key and nobody knew where he was. The tea ladies got into a right tizzy, as only tea ladies do when someone keeps them away from their teapot, and the umpires were not too pleased when they got to the middle and discovered they had only one set of bails. Clearly the missing Fred had to be found, and while the tea ladies went off on a search, the future flower of our national game improvised by taking off the bails at the end of every over and setting them down at the batsman's end with the gentle care of a priest baptizing an infant's head.

The occasion was the game between the Under 13s of Oxfordshire and Berkshire, and I was in attendance as a Proud Parent because Number Two son, leg break and googly bowler and Eating Champion of Berkshire and the South-West, was playing for his county. Even without one set of bails the setting was perfect: a cluster of dark green trees, a line of willows, the boats drifting along the nearby Thames and a church steeple at deep third man. We might not have the best players in the world, but we do have the most beautiful grounds.

By the time they'd found Fred and got the deckchairs out Oxfordshire had lost a quick wicket, but the new batsman was playing some lovely shots from under the brim of his sun hat. He was greatly helped by some old-fashioned field placings which revived the positions of point and long stop. Dr Grace would have approved, particularly of long stop, apart from his distressing habit of picking his nose during his inactive moments.

By the time Number Two son was called upon to perform, Oxfordshire were steaming along quite nicely. It was at this point that I began to debate the wisdom of parents watching their children in important cricket matches. My old man watched every game I ever played in, and I used to pretend I wished he'd stay away. And yet, when I went to the middle, the first thing I did after taking guard was not survey the field but search the spectators for a sight of him. I felt naked if I couldn't see him.

Not being a shrinking violet he was not the slightest abashed about letting people know that the clown in the middle, trying to late cut off his middle stump, was his son who, what is more, would get his backside kicked if he tried that 'fancy stuff' again. I can close my eyes and picture him behind the bowler's arm, always in my line of vision, and I can hear him groan at a piece of bad cricket and remember his cry of 'that's more like it' when I did something of which he approved.

In a sense the boy removing his sweater and measuring out his run was living testimony of my old man's love of cricket. It was he who coached him from the age of five, showed him how to hold a cricket ball, dissuaded him from every schoolboy's ambition to bowl fast and made him into a slow bowler. It was the same extraordinary Yorkshire-man who showed him how to bowl leg breaks and googlies reasoning that because Number Two son's parents had been daft enough to have him born outside of The County he might one day play against them and, as any idiot knows, Yorkshire cricketers don't like playing leg spin and googly bowlers.

Anyway, Grandad and chief coach would not have approved of his protégé's first over. In fact he would have thrown a fit. The lad was nervous and tensed up and bowled short. Second over he improved and started tossing it up. The next over he bowled two out of the back of the hand which turned a lot and had me smiling with pleasure. Overcome by his own genius he then bowled a long-hop which the batsman pulled with a crack like a starting pistol to mid-wicket where a languid West Indian took a catch with quite staggering nonchalance from a shot which would have had most club cricketers of my acquaintance diving the other way.

It was his only success and when the forty overs were ended Oxfordshire had scored 159 which was a few short of the numbers of sandwiches the tea ladies with their intimate knowledge of young boys' eating habits, gained perhaps from some hidden grounding in Greyfriars, had prepared for instant demolition. Number Two son polished off sixteen sandwiches and five pieces of cake, which, on a quick appraisal of the situation, seemed about normal.

The swot with specs glanced, cut and deflected.

The unique digestive system of young boys being what it is, the game re-started on time and Berkshire, like Oxfordshire, lost a quick wicket. But then a young lad, so small he seemed to peer over the top of his pads and, wearing the kind of spectacles that would automatically brand him as a 'swot', came to the wicket, and from the moment he played the first ball you knew he was a cricketer.

He was joined by another whose approach to the game of cricket was as uninhibited as the swot's was studious. The boy with specs glanced, cut and deflected, his bat as straight as a guardsman's back. The other carved about him. The Oxfordshire out-cricket, always tidy, became spectacular. One boy stopped an off-drive with his face and was carried from the field prostrate like an ancient warrior on his shield. His mum had kittens.

Then a young lad from Oxfordshire, bowling left arm over quick enough to make several watching fathers wince, found his rhythm and went through the Berkshire side. Number Two son went second ball to a leg stump yorker, the studious one was similarly underdone and very soon the Under 13s of Oxfordshire had accounted for the Berkshire side.

While all this was going on at Abingdon the West Indies scored 437 in a day against England at Headingley, but I had no doubt that I was in the right place.

Going home Number Two son was not very happy about being bowled without scoring. I tried to cheer him up.

'Remember Len Hutton started with a duck,' I said.

'Yes, and he didn't have to bat with bellyache like I did,' he said.

'That's true,' I said. 'What is more Len Hutton couldn't bowl a googly either.'

And we drove home through the sun-bleached Thames Valley with the evening birds swooping. As we did so the future of English cricket was curing his bellyache and his disappointment with a pound of fruit gums.

12 Yorkshire v West Indies, June 1976

Two minutes after we had started to digest the pork pies one Friday lunchtime a large West Indian named Wayne Daniel made a terrible mess of Arthur Robinson's stumps, and what had seemed in prospect a famous victory became an honourable defeat.

Over three days of high sunshine, intimidating fast bowling and courageous batting, two sides had fashioned a cricket match of rare quality, and no one who was there will forget it in a hurry. In the end Yorkshire lost to the West Indies by twenty runs on a wicket which their quick bowlers would no doubt love to have parcelled up and delivered to every ground they played on during the rest of the tour.

In the beer tent where all the wiseacres gathered, Ellis Robinson, who played in the great Yorkshire side of the thirties, reckoned that Herbert Sutcliffe would have won the game for Yorkshire 'off his cock box'. Someone asked how.

'Well, he could hook,' said Ellis.

'But they'd have set a man deep to catch him,' the man said.

'They'd have had to have been in the next county to catch Herbert,' said Ellis.

He was standing in a group containing Fred Trueman, Ray Illingworth and Johnny Wardle. Only one of the trio was sorry he wasn't out in the middle playing. Fred fancied his chances. 'Out theer,' he said, indicating the middle, 'tha needn't bother about bowling fast. Just straight will do.'

As he was talking Michael Holding bowled a ferocious bouncer at Chris Old. 'Did they ever bowl bouncers at you, Fred?' a punter asked.

'If they did they only did it once,' said Fred.

He recalled the time playing in the Home Counties when he was bowled two bouncers by a young and novice quick bowler who had been put up to it by a couple of the senior members of the side. Fred was already on the front foot expecting his proper dues from a fellow, if budding, member of the Fast Bowlers Union, when the ball whizzed passed his chin end.

He gazed unbelievingly down the wicket at the young fast bowler who glared at him menacingly. The two senior practical jokers were flat on their backs with laughter. The next ball was delivered, with Fred once more confidently on the front foot, having given the young bowler the benefit of the doubt, and again the ball pitched short and just missed his head.

The fast bowler glowered, but this time Fred acted. He walked down the track, attending to the turf, until he reached his belligerent opponent. Out of the corner of his mouth he said: 'Now tell me lad, does tha' want to die young?' The bowler must have understood the menace in the question because he went on to a long and fruitful county career. It could, however, have been one of the shortest on record.

Listening to the Yorkshire greats of other and vintage years yarning, one was reminded irresistibly of a different era when a match at Sheffield against the touring side meant Bramall Lane and the toughest audience anywhere in the world. It was cricket played in the setting of a great industrial city and the ground perfectly mirrored the society it represented.

Not long ago they stopped playing cricket at Bramall Lane and Sheffield United stuck a football stand on the grass where I had seen Lindwall bowl and Worrell bat. Last season Sheffield United was relegated to the Second Division, and it served them right for such a blasphemy.

Since then, Yorkshire cricket at Sheffield has been played at Abbeydale Park; a greater contrast is impossible to imagine. The setting is picture postcard in its intensity of beauty. Banks of high, green trees frame one end, and at the other the ground undulates seductively down to a row of marquees.

It has as much in common with Bramall Lane as a fair mountain to a muck heap, and yet no one, except those with long memories and those called upon to bat on it, could object to what happened in this game.

There might, I fancy, have been a different clamour from the crowd at Bramall Lane given the site of the West Indians bobbing and weaving as Old, Robinson and Sidebottom gave them a taste of their own medicine. There would, I know, have been a greater tension in the audience as Yorkshire fought so valiantly to beat the tourists.

And there would certainly have been more salty quotes to savour as the sun grew higher and the beer ran out. The only worthwhile one I heard was the spectator complaining about the ale.

'Thirty pence a pint, disgusting,' he said.

'Nay that's not much,' his mate said.

'It is if it's been supped once already,' he replied.

It was a game where the deeds on the field mattered more than the peripheral comings and goings. On the last day, when Yorkshire could so easily have won, Wayne Daniel bowled with the speed of light to rip the heart out of the Yorkshire batting. Holding at the other end beguiled the senses with his lissome approach but it was Daniel, rugged, muscular and unremittingly hostile, who looked the straighter and the better bowler.

The two of them threw up a challenge which would have

tested the bravest heart and the Yorkshire team met it unflinchingly. Youngy Athey, only eighteen and looking every inch a cricketer, was twice felled by fearsome blows from Daniel but still went doggedly into line and never flinched.

He played one cover-drive from the same bowler, which is the sort of shot only class cricketers make under that kind of pressure; and if this man doesn't make thousands of runs for Yorkshire in the very near future then my name is E. W. Swanton.

At the end the West Indians and the Yorkshire team gathered together in a tent for the expected drink and an unexpected free copy of Fred Trueman's new book. The tourists carried with them the confident swagger of an unbeaten team, and, moreover, a team that will take some beating.

On the other hand they came near to the brink at Abbeydale last week. 'We nearly stuffed you,' said one Yorkshire fan as the West Indians filed to their bus. It was true what he said. It would have been the perfect game of cricket, if only the result had been different.

13 Forty Not Out

When I was young and daft as a brush they sent for me to serve my country. Dressed in khaki I spent more time handling a cricket bat than a rifle. Indeed, the most offensive weapon I ever handled in the army was an ancient Imperial typewriter which occasionally shed one of its parts when in action. I always imagined the telegram being sent home: 'We regret to inform you that your son was mortally wounded by a piece of flying typeface. He departed bravely defending the typing pool.'

While in the army I played mostly for a Salisbury side which might not have been the best cricket team in the world but would have won the world championship for supping ale. In those days I hardly touched the stuff, being too much the conscientious athlete, but the rest of the team made up for my deficiencies.

I took the lads back to the mess one Saturday night after the game. I used to have the place to myself at weekends because all my brother officers were up in London pulling birds or such like. The steward used to knock off early on Saturdays and leave the bar open with a book of chitties to be signed on the honour system. I woke up next morning under the bar surrounded by empty bottles. My team-mates had drunk the place dry, done in about fifty quid's worth of booze.

The senior officer sent for me and asked how I imagined

I might pay the bill. 'Rob a bank?' I suggested. He shook his head and packed me off to live in a pub where they traded drink for cash and hadn't heard of the honour system.

One day, as I was leaving my new home to play an important game against a team from Hampshire, the landlord lured me from the straight and narrow by suggesting I sample some newly purchased wine. I turned up at the game tipsy and freed from all inhibitions played an innings in the manner of the great Garfield Sobers, scoring eighty-odd.

Later, as I sat in the pavilion hung over and not knowing whether to feel elated or ashamed, the skipper of the opposing side asked me to go to Southampton and play for the Hampshire Club and Ground side against a team skippered by C. J. Knott.

I went back to being a dedicated athlete. I retired early to bed, practised at the nets until I ran out of bowlers and laid off the demon booze. The day of the match I turned up at the County Ground at Southampton clear-eyed, brimming with health and full of cricket. The day was superb, the track flawless and the opposition ripe for the plucking- or so I was led to believe.

I went in first wicket down with about sixty odd on the board and was bowled first ball by C. J. Knott.

So much for sobriety.

I played once or twice with that team and made a few. In fact I nearly had a crack at making cricket my career but one or two things interfered, like Suez and my old man.

I was asked to play for Hampshire seconds (I think it was against Gloucester at Bristol) but the War Office decided I'd be better employed carrying a typewriter in Egypt. When I returned I told my old man that I was thinking about playing cricket full time.

'Who for?' he asked.

'Hampshire, if they'll have me,' I said.

'It's not like playing for Yorkshire lad, is it?' he said.

He was right.

All that and more came back to me the other day when someone reminded me it would be my fortieth birthday in a couple of weeks' time. What they said was: 'It's about time you took up golf.' Ignoring the advice but seeking the reason for it, I decided it must be my age.

I have arrived at that time of life when most of my contemporaries leave home and live at the golf club. They finick and fuss about grips and swings until they see me yawning and then they kindly change the subject.

Anyway, it set me thinking: reaching forty does seem to have that effect on people. Supposing all that time ago I had taken up cricket as a career, I would now be retired. Certainly all those young men who played with me that day at Southampton are no longer in county cricket. Where are they now? Probably playing golf.

Where am I now? Not doing too badly, thank you very much.

And yet....

It might have been a lovely life. Cricket all day long, languid days of high summer, the pain and the pleasure of the greatest of games. I'm still playing of course. Not quite county standard but it will do.

As I reach my fortieth birthday I have only one resolution, which is to keep on playing cricket until they carry me off. At a time of life when many take up other sports such as golf, bowls, shove ha'penny, mixed bathing or visiting health farms, I am simply resolved to go on playing cricket.

Nowadays I partake of a small libation before attending the crease. It no longer has the effect of freeing my inhibitions: it simply enables me to reach the middle without incident.

So while others worry about their handicap, join sports centres or attend gymnasiums in an effort to come to terms with the middle years, you'll find me propped up at the wicket, a willing slave to the 'Sovran King of Sports'. I can think of no better way, or better company in which to grow old gracefully.

14 Keystone Cricket

The Vic Lewis Cricket Club is to cricket what the Keystone Cops were to the forces of law and order. Its members prove the theory that humour is the grotesque disparity between human aspiration and human achievement. For those of you who may be unaware of its existence, I should explain that it is a motley assembly of show-business people who every Sunday enact their secret fantasies to be Dennis Lillee, Sir Garfield Sobers or a modest mixture of the two. They do so in the name of charity and under the benign leadership of the aforesaid Mr Lewis, whose love for the game surpasseth all understanding.

Having played for Mr Lewis for a few seasons I feel I must counter the slur that his team plays what is commonly termed 'comic cricket'. This criticism causes great hurt to a dedicated body of athletes whose general aim is to look like proper cricketers. That we sometimes fall short of that ambition and that the results are often hilarious is something we are working on at present.

In the meantime let the knockers take note of the fact that we are unbeaten against club sides this season. To be honest I must admit that this triumphant march has a lot to do with the fact that our opponents are warned of the consequences should they be foolish enough to win. Nonetheless we are a winning side, and the dressing room resounds with the badinage of happy and successful athletes.

Of the county sides we have thus far encountered only Surrey have defeated us, and they have received a stern

warning as to their future conduct. Our most memorable match this season was against Warwickshire, at Edgbaston in Dennis Amiss's benefit game. This ended in a tie, and while I am proud to have been a member of that great team effort I must confess to being exceedingly disappointed with my personal performances on that auspicious day.

It was, in fact, a traumatic experience I suffered and to understand its gravity it is necessary to comprehend the nature of the games we play. I have already explained that our team must win. Also written into our contract is that we all get a bowl and a bat during the course of a game, and moreover, are allowed to impress our wives and children by scoring at least twenty-five runs when we play the county sides. This last deception is necessary because it stifles all those boring family arguments about: 'What is a man of your age doing walking to the wicket in front of all those people carrying a piece of wood?' which become so tedious after a time.

Therefore, having travelled all the way to play against the men of Warwickshire, I was sustained by the knowledge that I would score at least twenty or thirty runs on my Edgbaston debut. Warwickshire batted first and with the score at something like a hundred and odd for one wicket my captain decided that enough was enough by asking me to bowl. Facing me as I delivered my first over was Alvin Kallicharran, the well-known scourge of bowlers. I was unimpressed. Having watched him closely as he thrashed Lillee and Co. all over the park in Test matches and the like I knew that if he had a weakness it was against a long hop that bounced twice.

And so it proved. My second ball pitched half way down the wicket lifted wearily and invited the hook shot. Kallicharran fell for it and whirled his bat not knowing that the ball was going to bounce once more before rolling on to his middle stump. I took the acclaim of my team mates with becoming modesty, explaining how I couldn't imagine why the England lad didn't bowl that way at him. Next I was faced with the redoubtable John Jameson who succumbed to a leg side full-toss which was caught by a man I had especially positioned in the road outside of the ground.

My figures of two for fifty from five overs were satisfactory proof of the virtues of line and length and helped keep the Warwickshire total down to a reasonable 376 in just over two hours. We were undaunted by the score knowing, that if we lost, the next Warwickshire player due a benefit would have to find another show-biz team to play against.

Thus, in optimistic frame of mind I accepted my captain's invitation to open the innings. Having opened at Headingley, The Oval and Lord's in the past and knowing now as I did then, that I was guaranteed a few runs, I walked to the wicket with proud and confident stride.

I was a little doubtful about Bob Willis marking out his full run as I prepared to take strike, and I knew the worst when the first ball, delivered at great pace, hit my bat before I had commenced the back lift. I thought of having a word with his captain, but Yorkshire pride made me grit my teeth and peer hopefully down the wicket.

The next ball shattered my dreams (and the social contract that exists between Mr Lewis's team and the opposition). Some say it was a yorker, others that it was a full toss. I don't know because I didn't see it. What I did see was my middle peg flattened and a big O against my name on the scoreboard.

That was how I became the first player ever in Mr Lewis's team to get a duck in a first-class fixture. It also explains how I came to have words with Mr Willis some time later. I merely informed him of my unavailability for his benefit matches whenever that might be. Drowning my sorrows in the bar I was approached by my youngest son who had been autograph hunting. On one page he had Alvin Kallicharran's signature and underneath, in his childish hand, he had written, 'My Dad bowled him out.'

Already I am looking forward to next season, full of fantasy and hope. Thus, in our darkest hour we are sustained by the innocence of little children.

15 Sex and Sport

During a recent MCC tour of Australasia, our players were told that they could spend no more than twenty-one nights with their wives. Had the tour lasted only a fortnight this would have been fair enough, but as it went on for five months, the hard rations imposed on the team would have driven a eunuch to distraction, never mind a lusty athlete seeking his wife's fond embrace.

No wonder we did so badly. It wasn't Thomson and Lillee who caused the problems. Our lads were too preoccupied crossing off the days until they were on a promise to bother too much about cricket.

Sex once more rears its ugly head in sport, and I am glad to see the Marylebone Clodpoles Club, quick thinking as ever, is going to do something about it. The rule was made by a committee of the Test and County Cricket Board, whose secretary, Mr D. B. Carr, is quoted as saying that the ruling would be reviewed before the next MCC tour.

That is one MCC meeting I would love to attend. Presumably the players and their wives will be called to give evidence.

'Excuse me, Mrs Titmus, but was twenty-one days enough?'

'Speak for yourself, cheekie.'

The team physiotherapist, Bernard Thomas, was the man who enforced the rule in Australia, so undoubtedly he

will become a key figure in the committee's deliberations.

D. B. Carr: 'Tell me, Mr Thomas, from your point of view, how the team did on tour.'

Mr Thomas: 'I am delighted to say, sir, that the tour was a complete and utter success. Team discipline was superb and there were several splendid all-round performances. Top averages were Mr and Mrs Knott with twenty-one nights and no complaints, followed closely by Mr and Mrs Titmus with eighteen nights not out.'

D. B. Carr: 'Thank you Mr Thomas, and I am sure the Committee would like placed on record our thanks to you for doing such a splendid job in the most trying circumstances.'

Cries of 'hear, hear!' and a short burst of 'For He's a Jolly Good Fellow'.

I have never understood the puritan ethic about sex and sport. The notion that it weakens the man is absurd and has been scientifically shown to be so. But still the feeling persists that it is bad for the athlete. I would have thought the opposite was true, that it benefited the athlete because it relaxed him, calmed his frustrations. Certainly the frustrated and randy athlete is not likely to give of his best. I know; I speak from bitter experience.

When I was a young man and serving my Queen in her armed forces (at her insistence and not mine, I might add) I played for a team of ruffians in the West Country whose idea of getting match-ready was a quick net on a Friday night followed by a good booze-up. It was after one of these training sessions that I succumbed to the charms of a voluptuous barmaid called Elsie, or some such, who also fell for my charming ways and accompanied me on a midnight tour of the river bank.

We were doing very nicely, thank you very much, when our passion was interrupted by someone shining a torch on us. 'Who are you?' I asked, feebly.

'Police Constable Horace Pepper,' he said, the light unwavering in my eyes. I began to get used to the beam and to see through it and round it. I said, 'Tell me, if you are Police Constable Horace Pepper, where is your helmet and why are you not wearing trousers.' Whereupon he turned and belted along the river bank with me in pursuit giving credence to the immortal line by Confucious that Man with Trousers Down Cannot Catch Man with No Pants. It later turned out that the imposter was a notable voyeur who got his jollies by patrolling that part of the river.

All right for him, but what about me? Elsie was in no mood to further our relationship after such a traumatic experience, and I was left frustrated and raring to go. Next day I played like a big jessie, all tense and nervous, while my opening partner, who'd had a skinful and then gone home to his lovely wife, batted like a dream and scored a ton.

Which only goes to prove what I have always believed, that sex and sport do mix, and if MCC had any sense they'd pay for the wives and girlfriends to accompany the players on tour, and instruct Bernard Thomas that any player not taking advantage of this extra facility be sent home for not trying.

The whole silly business was summed up for me by the story of a county player whose captain was a fitness fanatic. He was constantly lecturing his players about abusing their bodies, and the dangers of sex. They could never accuse him of not practising what he preached, because it was well known that in his playing days he slept in the spare room during the cricket season, only sharing a bed with his wife during the football season.

Anyway, one day this joker was taking a team talk when, inevitably, he got on to the subject of sex and the athlete: 'I have discovered something that ought to put you all off sex during the cricket season. According to medical research, making love is like running seven-and-a-half miles. In other words, it knackers you.'

The team took all this in without comment until the next day, when they turned up for training on a wet and windy morning. They lined up on the road.

'What's the form today?' said my mate to the captain.

'Running,' said the captain.

'How far?' asked my mate.

'Seven-and-a-half miles,' said the captain.

'Couldn't we have a quick one instead?' asked my mate.

16 Jockstrap Joys

Alec rang the other day to see if I'd take over from poor Dennis Amiss. Normally I would have jumped at the chance, but I injured myself playing a two-day game against the Incogs last week. Normally I would spare you the details, but as I know a lot of young cricketers will read this book, I would be doing them a disservice if I didn't show them at least some of the pitfalls to be avoided.

My injury came about by a series of accidents, the first being that I agreed to play in the side after one of our regular players had called off because his granny had caught her toe in the mangle or some such daft excuse.

Our skipper, a kindly man, had never seen me play before, and laboured under the delusion that I was a bowler. Now, it is true I can turn my arm over, indeed some indication of my talent in this area can be seen from my list of victims for this season which includes such fine players as Mr Alvin Kallicharran of Warwickshire, and Miss Sue Lawley of 'Nationwide'. But I only bowl in emergencies and then at a gentle pace off a run-up remarkably like the great Illingworth's.

Therefore, imagine my consternation and horror when our skipper informed me I was opening the bowling and, what is more, with a new conker. I didn't dare tell him the truth because I didn't want to hurt his feelings. Instead I set about making the best of a bad job.

I calculated that apart from making an ass of myself, the next likeliest thing to happen was that I would disintegrate in the delivery stride. With this in mind I decided to wear my supporter which I believe is referred to in some quarters as a jockstrap. In any event it is cross between a body belt and a G-string and, tucking my shirt tightly into its elasticated grip, I took the field feeling suitably bolstered against the coming ordeal.

I measured out my run – eight paces and a hop – and prepared to bowl the first ball. Everything went well for the eight paces. Indeed, I remember thinking my approach was a fair copy of Garfield's glide to the crease. It was in the delivery stride that things went wrong. Unfortunately, I had tucked too much of my shirt into my jockstrap, and too tightly. Consequently I couldn't get my arm more than shoulder high without causing undue and painful tension.

Therefore, what should have been a climactic moment of delivery, left hand flung high and heavenwards, right arm whirling over in a full arc, developed into a catastrophic parody.

As my left arm went up, so did my jockstrap, causing my eyes to water. This reduced my ambition somewhat and ruined my aim. The ball was finally delivered from a crouching position with me giving a fair imitation of the Hunchback of Notre Dame. The batsman, not the slightest bit concerned with the high drama taking place before his eyes smote the ball to the boundary.

Our skipper looked incredulous, but he sympathized when I explained how the disaster came about and allowed me to make the necessary adjustments to my dress. Nonetheless, he kept giving me funny glances.

I never recovered from the effect of that first ball. My injury was traumatic rather than physical – 'shell-shocked' is the current jargon, I believe.

Anyway, I told Alec this, and he listened sympathetically enough and said he quite understood why I had to turn down the offer to bat at No. 4 for England. He said he

felt sure that Gubby would not hold it against me, and that I would have another chance before the end of the series.

I asked Alec if he had anyone else in mind for the position. He told me that Jack Hampshire was next on the list. I remarked that the Yorkshire player had been showing good form lately. Alec said it had nothing to do with form, simply that it was Jack's turn for England duty on the rota system. Alec explained that Gubby and the England selectors had used this system for a long time. Apparently Gubby got the idea from a chemist in St John's Wood. The system is strictly applied, which is how Colin got sent to Australia and not Jack and why Jack gets his chance now rather than Colin.

I asked if the same system applied to captains, because if it did it must be Closey's turn again soon. Alec said he didn't know too much about the captaincy because that was left to people like Gubby who understood these things.

I must say Alec seems a new man since our glorious draw at Lord's. He said that Tony was proving an inspiration both on the field and off, and that his English lessons were progressing nicely.

For my part, I pledged my undying support for Gubby and the stalwart band of men who have put English cricket in its present situation. To that end I promised Alec I would not jeopardize my own future, and that of my country, by indulging in any more pace bowling, with or without my jockstrap. We parted on the friendliest of terms, with many a jest about my mishap. How fortunate we are to have such a capable and experienced campaigner at the helm in our time of need.

As I face up to the pace attack of Knotty Green Second XI next weekend, I shall ruefully reflect that, but for the fickle finger of fate, I would have been facing Lillee and Co. at Headingley. Say what you like about Alec and Gubby, but there is no getting away from the fact that the way they pick teams anybody stands a chance of playing for England.

17 A Visit to Lord's

The nice thing about going to Lord's is that most people are genuinely surprised to see me there. It was most succinctly summed up last season by a member of the Marylebone Clodpoles Club who, on seeing me enter the Pavilion, clutched his throat and swooned clear away.

The fact is I like Lord's, even though I could do without some of the inhabitants. What is needed at Lord's is a simple exercise in social democracy. For a trial period of a month, say, the occupants of the Pavilion should be made to change places with the real fans who make all the noise in front of the Tavern.

In that way the Pavilion would be filled with fun and laughter for the only time in its long and mournful life and, what is more important, the members would be scragging the brewers for supplying the Tavern with the most insipid, flat, tasteless, gutless beer it has ever been my displeasure to drink. It is fit only to drown puppies in.

That is the only change I would make at Lord's, for it really is one of my favourite cricket grounds, and going there as I do every year, for the opening day of a new season, still fills me with a childlike, day-trip feeling in the early-morning sun. The last time I went the ground looked as fresh and crisp as a newly laundered sheet, and Willis and Ward bowled fast on a slow wicket. The tea lady coped manfully with a crowd of four people assembled at the

Tavern, and I stood next to a man who, with the simple addition of a pair of snow shoes, could have been dressed for an expedition to the Antarctic.

He told me he was in his seventies, and came every new season to Lord's to sniff the air. Together we watched as Davison of Leicestershire supremely confident and whippy-wristed, made us wish – not for the first time – that he was British. The old man was impressed. 'Another foreigner, though,' he said and shook his head sadly.

It was here, at Lord's in the free seats at the Nursery End, that I saw my first foreign player. He patrolled the covers with the indolent grace of the great athlete, and ran a man out with a swoop and a throw so fast that no one who saw it could swear that the ball he picked up on the run was the same that demolished the stumps with the batsman yards adrift. His name was Learie Constantine.

It was here, at Lord's, that I achieved one of my lifelong ambitions by walking through the Long Room wearing an MCC sweater. This was done for a wager during a charity cricket match which nearly marked the finish of Mr David Frost's career as a natural successor to Alan Knott. We had Mr Wesley Hall on our side, and as I believe in being nice to fast bowlers, whether they be on my own or the other side, I engaged him in conversation and discovered that he was fully recovered after a recent operation, and was bowling as fast as ever. What is more, he said he thought he might let it go for a few overs.

As we went out to field our esteemed wicket-keeper, the aforesaid Mr Frost, asked me if I had any information about Wes. I told him that he was recovering from an operation and wasn't likely to slip himself.

'Where do you think I should stand?' asked David.

'Not too far back,' I said.

Thus it came to pass, one Sunday afternoon at Lord's, that David Frost was no more than five yards from the stumps when Wesley Winfield Hall hurtled a cricket ball towards him at about 80 mph. It was a beamer so swift that even Mike Smith, the Middlesex opener, didn't move. Nor did Mr Frost, which is as well, because the ball scraped his right ear, travelling like a shell, before crashing first bounce into the boundary fence. White-faced, Mr Frost turned round to see first and second slip fifty yards back draped over the railings in postures of helpless laughter.

Nothing so funny, or dramatic, happened at Lord's on my last visit except that Davison reached his century in less time than it took the tea lady to serve her patient crowd of four customers. The old man left after lunch, presumably to get his balaclava. Ray Illingworth, who started his first-class career before some of his present team were born, looked like an advert for eternal youth and the refreshment bar near the Mound Stand ran out of tea at 4.15, which could only happen on an English cricket ground at the start of the season.

At the end of the day I stood by the Tavern and took stock. I was chilled to the marrow, cut in two by a keen wind, my fingers were like a parsnip, my nose was running, my belly was rumbling in protest at the ale, Illingworth was out, there wasn't a single Yorkshireman in the MCC side and I was surrounded by people in those funny ties. Yet I was the happiest man on the planet. A new cricket season was upon us, and that suited me for the next few months.

18 Cricket Characters

I remember going to see Nottinghamshire play Yorkshire when I was a lad. It must have been some time ago because Notts had a good team in those days and bowed the knee to no one. If memory is true the game was played at Bramall Lane and Nottinghamshire won the toss and batted. What I do remember clearly is that Notts opened with Keeton and Harris. Now they were a formidable pair, and Harris was not only a fine player but a man with an impish way of doing things.

He was in the habit of opening proceedings by hanging a 'Do Not Disturb' sign on his bails before taking first ball, and like a few of the greats Notts players – Gunn, Hardstaff and Simpson – was a player of infinite mood and zest. That day long ago he decided to bait the large and partisan Yorkshire crowd by demonstrating in the morning session the art of defensive play. He hardly scored a run before lunch and the louder the crowd booed the more grandiose became his defensive flourishes. He went to lunch on a fanfare of catcalls.

After lunch he took Yorkshire apart and finished up with a double century treating the crowd to a doff of the cap and a sweeping bow whenever, and however reluctantly, they applauded one magnificent shot after the other.

Modern-day cricketers could well argue that nowadays a pre-lunch sleep-in such as Harris promoted would have the pavilion burnt down and the square buried in beer cans. And they might be right because if it be true that on the whole today's cricketers have lost the grand manner of rebuking their critics, it is for certain that today's crowds have similarly lost the art of telling the players where to get off.

Arthur 'Ticker' Mitchell, who ruined many a Roses game for a Lancastrian, will bear witness to this. He was playing in a Yorkshire *v* Lancashire game at Old Trafford and doing his duty by staying there and scoring nothing when play was interrupted by a voice from the popular side.

'Mitchell,' the voice yelled, in aggrieved tones. 'Mitchell, I want tha' to know that every Bank Holiday I come here to see t' cricket and every Bank Holiday, bare none, tha' comes out and buggers it up for me. Mitchell, I've had enough, I'm going home and I'm not coming back…ever.'

The saddest decline in modern cricket is the relationship between opposing teams. During MCC's recent games against Australia we have heard much of the 'verbalizing' that goes on during the Test matches, and, although we only get the expurgated version there can be little doubt that the on-field chat between the players is not that which passed for pertinent, or proper, when W. G. was in his pomp.

The point is, of course, that today's bad-mouth brigade are incapable of understanding the nuance of the oblique statement. Take a straightforward example. Today's batsman is likely greeted with the news that the opposing quickie is going to knock his f…… head off. A few years ago things were different.

My old man told a story of playing against a fast bowler of exceptional pace. After the first over when my old man literally did not see one delivery he confided to the stumper, 'By heck, but yon bloke's quick.'

'True,' said the stumper, 'but tha' should have seen him before he were gassed.'

But the best example of psychological warfare in cricket concerns the elderly judge playing for the local village side. The opening batsman of the opposing team hit the ball into the rhododendrons at square leg and the judge trotted off in pursuit. He disappeared into the bushes and about three minutes elapsed before he emerged with the ball.

At tea the judge seemed broody, and to break his mood the skipper gently kidded him about being long in the bushes.

'What kept you?' he asked.

'Well, to tell the truth when I went into the rhododendrons to retrieve the ball I came upon a couple making love. I had to ask them to move over in order to get the ball. Most distressing,' said the judge.

'Oh, come now,' said the skipper, 'you're a man of the world. Surely you're not upset at seeing two people making love.'

'It's not that at all,' said the judge. 'It did not upset me seeing the fellow on the job – but I must, confess I was very upset when the bounder came in at number seven.'

Present-day cricketers could learn much from that true story. The moral is there are more ways of getting at the crowd and your opponents than giving the V-sign. Perhaps all is not lost. Not long ago Harvey-Walker, the Derbyshire batsman, announced his opinion of a brutal wicket at Buxton by striding to the middle and handing over his false teeth to the square leg umpire. He was out in rapid fashion whereupon, with massive dignity, he collected his molars and replaced them in his mouth, before making his way back to the pavilion.

I think Harvey-Walker would have loved playing with Mr Harris who never overstepped the line dividing good-natured teasing of your opponents and bad-tempered abuse. Sometimes, during a long innings – and he played many for Notts – the game would be interrupted while a minion bearing a telegram addressed to Harris and marked 'Most Urgent' walked to the wicket.

Harris would open the telegram, read it, dismiss the messenger and resume play against opponents much disconcerted by the unusual interruption and consumed with curiosity as to the contents of a telegram so urgent it had to be delivered to a fellow on a cricket field.

Had they inquired of the recipient the nature of the message they would have found it read: 'WELL DONE SO FAR BUT KEEP GOING YOU FOOL, signed C. HARRIS.' Sending telegrams to himself was not a mark of Harris's eccentricity, rather a demonstration of his belief that of all games cricket is the one best suited to the man of wit and style and a plague on the oafs and dullards.

19 The Debut

The first time you play cricket with the big boys is like your first love affair or the first taste of shandy on a sweaty day – something you will remember for the rest of your life. I go back thirty years to the time I walked onto a cricket field with what my father always called 'proper' cricketers, which is to say men who didn't muck about on the field of play.

I can remember it vividly to this day: I can recall the dressing room smell of sweat and liniment and linseed oil, I can see the clothes hanging on the nails that served as pegs, and I remember my heroes one by one. The local hitter was Mr Roberts. He had a false leg and I often wondered what it looked like. Well, I found out that day they played me in the first team. The other hitter, Mr Stewardson, had a bat bound in brown leather and tacked up the back of the blade. He used to clout the ball immense distances and attributed his success to the bat which he had used for ten years or more. When asked about the binding he would look around him in conspiratorial fashion to make sure that no one else was listening and whisper 'Kangaroo skin, tha' sees.' The questioner would nod wisely as if it was common knowledge that kangaroo skin on a cricket bat would make the ball leap from its surface.

Mr Berry was our spin bowler and probably the most gifted player in the side. He bowled leg breaks at about

Underwood's pace and, when the mood took him, was unplayable. What I always wanted to know about him, however, was how he kept his sleeves up when he bowled. As someone who always contrived to look like an unmade bed after six overs in the field, I was envious of Mr Berry's ability to play through the longest and hottest day with not a ruffle in his outline and not a shirtsleeve out of place. I watched him dress but never did find out the secret and dared not ask him in case he thought I was daft, or a wrong 'un, or both.

The quick bowlers were my old man and Mr Baker who had the longest run in local cricket. It was nothing for him to start his run from behind the sightscreen and on one ground, where there was a gate behind the bowler's arm, he actually started outside the field, bursting onto the scene like a runaway horse. Actually he had a gliding, smooth approach to the wicket and was a good-looking man with a handsome profile, and a liking for curved pipes and gentle conversation. By comparison his opening partner, my old man, was a volatile and explosive cricketer who expected, nay demanded, a wicket with every ball he bowled and woe betide any fielder with trembling fingers who stood between him and his ambition.

Our wicket-keeper was called Minty and he was a huge man with a bald head and a look of Telly Savalas. He wore the biggest protector I have ever seen, and he needed to because he stood up to every bowler no matter what the pace or the state of the wicket. His simple theory of wicket-keeping was that the job involved stopping a cricket ball with any part of the anatomy available which accounted for his extra large protector and the bruises that covered him from head to foot after every game.

Those were a few of the people I shared the pavilion with some thirty years ago on a hot August day when I made my debut with the local side. I was eleven or twelve at the time, a tin-tack in amongst the six-inch nails. I knew I wouldn't get a bat or a bowl and that I mustn't make a mistake in the

field or else I'd get murdered by the old man when I got home. On paper it seems a daunting prospect, but to me at that time it was the highlight of my life.

Two things happened in the game to convince me that I was right to want to be Len Hutton. The first was that someone swore on the field, using a word that in those days you would never use in front of eleven-year-old innocents. I looked quickly at my old man to see his reaction, but he just looked at me and winked, and I knew at that moment that I had been accepted into the brotherhood of cricketers and was not an impostor.

But the most marvellous moment came when I made a catch. It was a straightforward effort but I held it, and I knew they'd have to put my name on the score book and there would be proof of my existence. Moreover there was a chance I might get a mention in the local paper, but it didn't happen. Mind you I made up for the lack of publicity much later when I was working as a reporter on the local paper and also playing cricket every weekend.

Then I wrote my own reports and became the best publicized player in South Yorkshire. Headlines like: 'PARKINSON AGAIN' or 'ANOTHER PARKINSON TRIUMPH' were a commonplace in our local paper and even in the lean times the readers were guaranteed a 'PARKINSON FAILS' headline every now and again just to keep the name fresh in their minds.

All these memories came drifting deliciously back when my nine-year-old was asked to make his debut with the local club. The other two were already veterans, having been blooded young, but the little one I was holding back on the advice of his Uncle Geoff who had been working on the forward defensive stroke and Uncle Illy who had been showing how to get side-on in the delivery stride.

We knew of his selection the day before the game but didn't dare break the news to him until the next morning in order for him to sleep in untroubled peace. Otherwise the only way we could have persuaded him to have closed his eyes was by giving him a bottle of sleeping tablets and half a bottle of scotch. He took the field looking like an advert for soap powder and a quick check around the field revealed that the only other participants smaller than him were the stumps.

He was hidden by the captain (who happened to be his elder bother acting on my instructions) in all the places where you don't expect a cricket ball to go whereupon, inevitably, the opposition hit the ball to all those places where you don't expect a cricket ball to go. Still, he fielded well and earned my particular admiration for sensibly going the other way to a fierce top edge that would have given Derek Randall trouble.

But his big moment came when he had to come in at number two to play out the last over. The opposition kindly looped gentle spin at him whereby he nearly decapitated short leg with a brusque pull off the middle of his bat. He came off flushed as a drunken sailor with three not out, and I immediately informed Alec of his availability. That was on a Monday. On Friday before he went to school I saw him looking at the sports pages in the local paper, and I knew what he was seeking. He looked in vain. I couldn't tell him what I knew, that you don't need a yellowed cutting to remind you of your first game with proper cricketers. It is burned in your mind forever.

20 Fire and Brimstone

Fast bowlers are set apart from their fellow men by a mixture of fear, envy, grudging respect and slack-mouthed admiration. In the whole of sport only the heavyweight champion of the world commands the same clutch of reactions. They carry with them on the field of play the threat of sudden violence. They are the men who probe the taproots of technique, lay bare the nerve endings. As Maurice Leyland once observed (and we must never tire of quoting the classics): 'None of us like 'em, but not all of us lets on.'

Being the son of a fast bowler I know more than a little about them. If I grew up nervous of the quickies it was only because I lived with one for a considerable length of time and although, contrary to common rumour, my old man did not eat raw meat, he undoubtedly meant business when he had a cricket ball in his hand.

Like all fast bowlers, he didn't mind whom he hit or where he hit them. Any fast bowler, if he is honest, will admit to the same attitude, and if he says different he is probably changing sex and will likely end up playing in frilly drawers with Rachel Heyhoe Flint as his captain. I am not saying that it is necessary for a fast bowler to be a homicidal maniac, but it certainly helps.

My old man was the gentlest of souls off the field, but when striding in to rocket the ball at his opponent he didn't

really care whether he knocked over the batsman or the wickets.

He wasn't exactly popular in certain neighbouring villages where he left a trail of sore limbs and bruised reputations. Nor was he immune from counter-attack. As a child I remember the crowd cheering as father was carried off after being felled by the local fast bowler who repaid a broken rib from a previous encounter by hitting my old man straight between the eyes.

For a week or so thereafter he sported the most spectacular pair of black eyes outside the Panda House at London Zoo. It didn't seem to bother him too much. 'I'll bet you yon fast bowler doesn't turn up at our ground,' was all he said. And he was right, the excuse being that the fast bowler's Uncle Willy had taken a turn for the worse and needed looking after.

The presence of a really fast bowler in a team has always guaranteed a selection problem for the other side. Many's the captain who has been told on the eve of a game that one or more of his batsmen have poorly grannies or upset stomachs. Speaking personally I don't think I have ever run away from an encounter with a quick bowler, but it is also undeniably true that all my best and bravest innings against genuine pace have been played in the club bar.

I was lucky in that all the years I have played cricket, no matter what the level or the state of the track, I have never been injured, which probably argues much for my technique against pace consisting as it does of playing from a position somewhat adjacent to the square leg umpire.

Even that technique is not infallible because although it has served me well it did not prevent one of my former opening partners getting hit on every square inch of his person. He was the most accident-prone cricketer I have ever seen.

I cannot remember one game in the three seasons I played with him when he did not suffer some disaster. And if he didn't sustain an injury in the middle he would compensate by falling off his bike going home. His injuries were so frequent and varied that the local St John's Ambulance Brigade instructor used to pick him up every Monday and take him down to the village hall to let his students practice on him.

He was known as 'W. C.' because of the amount of time he spent in that establishment prior to facing a quick bowler. I used to have to knock on the door to tell him it was time to go to the middle whereupon he would emerge wan and trembling to face his weekly encounter with disaster.

He wore more protection than a medieval knight and was the only player I knew who wore two groin protectors – one a lightweight batsman's job and the other a monstrous stumper's affair which covered every part of his lower abdomen.

I was present the day he was struck in that most protected part of his body by a fast bowler of immense pace. As he lay on the floor he indicated in somewhat robust terms that the blow had trapped a certain part of his anatomy between the two boxes. The bowler took the news phlegmatically enough: 'Looks like a job for t'fire brigade then, he said.

The thought of being attended to by fire officers wearing brass helmets and wielding oxyacetylene equipment proved too much for W. C., who retired to his favourite room in the pavilion in order to supervize his own emergency operation. I often wonder what went on at the local ambulance class the following Monday.

Fast bowlers make things happen because they deal in fire and spectacle. They are the flamboyant swank-pots of cricket because they carry the ultimate deterrent. Often this sense of power sends them queer in the head. For instance I knew one black quickie of fearsome pace and reputation who earned a living as a bus driver and became so convinced of his reputation as the local superman that he would not stop to pick up passengers if there was a white man at the bus stop. Thus he would often tour the town all day without stopping, his clippie snoozing contentedly on the top deck.

But generally we should forgive fast bowlers anything for they are to cricket what comets are to the heavens. Batsmen are more durable, slow bowlers have a duller and more lasting gleam, but the real speed merchants are here and gone leaving a brilliant memory trailed by a gasp of wonder.

Lillee, Thomson, Roberts, and Holding of the moderns similarly light up the present scene. On and off the field they are the centre of all attention, provoking that mixture of hostility and respect so peculiar to their breed. They handle the situation well because the fastest bowler in the world, like the best fighter, doesn't have to prove a thing in a street brawl.

I remember standing in a bar with Fred Trueman when a man shoved a tatty piece of paper under his nose, 'twixt pint and lips and said, rudely, 'Sign that.' Fred lowered his pint, slowly looked the man up and down. The man got the message. 'Would you mind very much signing your auto-graph, please, Mr Trueman,' he said. Fred did so without saying a word.

Once, I tried the same tactic. Coming off the field from a charity game a youth roughly grabbed my arm and stuck an autograph book under my nose. 'Put yer name on it,' he commanded. I gave him Fred's look. 'Blimey,' he said, 'Yer look like my bleedin' probation officer.'

21 Away from Home

Like women who kiss and run, sporting tours promise much but give nothing. It is as true of the international tour as it is of the local club tour. The only thing our footballers learned when they ventured to Mexico was how to do the Aztec Two-step to combat Montezuma's Revenge. Similarly, our lads in the West Indies become adept at the Trinidadian Turkey-trot in avoidance of the Caribbean Cruise.

The local club tour is similarly fraught. To start with, the basic premise of these tours is a damnable lie. Club members talk themselves into believing that they are going on tour to play cricket or rugby or whatever against some good opposition. In fact a group of men are running away from wives and girlfriends to get drunk and, if possible, have a bit of skirt in a hayfield.

Drink is the serious problem, particularly on cricket tours, for it can be said without fear of contradiction that nothing yet devised by man is worse for a sick hangover than a day's cricket in the summer sun. The morning after the night before the most you can pray for is to win the toss and bat and hope to God that your openers will bat all day.

When we had to field first anything could happen, and sometimes did. I once saw our fast bowler, drunk as a squaddie at eleven in the morning, race in to deliver the first ball of the day, flatten the umpire at his end, crash through the wickets and deliver a beamer from ten yards down the pitch which all but decapitated the umpire at square leg. Moreover, he had the temerity to appeal, although we never did discover what for, nor whom he expected to judge his appeal, as both adjudicators were stretched flat on the turf.

He was led from the pitch, moaning gently, to be followed shortly by our wicket-keeper, who sat down during a drinks break and fell into a drunken slumber from which he refused to be roused.

On that same tour the stumper became involved in an incident that changed his whole life. We were touring Derbyshire, and we were having a farewell drink in Buxton before moving on to Matlock the next day. Our wicket-keeper, an argumentative drunk, became involved in a dispute with our scorer about who had the best sense of direction.

This somewhat aimless argument took on an altogether more meaningful aspect when the scorer bet the stumper he couldn't find his way at night on foot from Buxton to Matlock. The stumper accepted, and thus it was that one midsummer night, with the stars glinting, he set off with many a drunken farewell. His money had been taken from him to prevent his cheating by taking a taxi.

The next day we arrived in our bus at Matlock, and our stumper hadn't turned up. Later on we phoned the law because we were worried about him. Three weeks later we had a letter from him postmarked Buenos Aires, saying that he had met this dusky beauty and intended to marry her, and would we send his money because he'd need a few bob for the wedding.

Another problem with tours is that, on the whole, the opposition is likely to be the kind that can't get fixtures with neighbouring clubs, which is why many of our opponents on tour were the inmates of various institutions, both penal and mental. It was while playing at one of the latter that I came across two of the most extraordinary

sporting characters I have ever met.

The first was an opening bat who wore only a single pad as he had one tin leg. He had a remarkable style which centred around his ability to strike the ball to all parts of the field, sometimes with his bat, but more often with his tin leg. This, of course, was in the days before the change of rule about leg-byes, and often he would score a quick thirty with all but ten coming from his leg.

Appealing for lbw was a waste of time because the two local umpires, both inmates of the same institution as the batsman, regarded it as a huge joke. For instance, in the first over, our opening bowler had a good delivery kicked off middle stump for four byes. The ball hitting the leg made a sound like a bell. He appealed loudly to the umpire, who thought for a moment and said, 'One o'clock and all's well.'

The same team had a fast bowler who wore a monocle and ran to the wicket with a ball in either hand. He was completely ambidextrous, so the batsman had no idea from which hand the ball was coming. His speciality was to bowl with both arms simultaneously, and he had an even subtler variation whereby he would deliver one ball off the wrong foot, followed a moment later by another delivery from a normal action.

Any batsman who exercised his right to inquire of the umpire what kind of delivery to expect was given the totally disarming answer: 'I'm blowed if I know.'

Anyone who has ever been on a sporting tour will know I am speaking the truth when I say that when it comes to playing away from home, sport imitates life in that we would be better off if we stayed in our own back yard.

22 Sporting Nig-Nogs

I came across my first sporting nig-nog in the army. His name was Quinn, and he was an extreme case being so unco-ordinated that although he could whistle and tie his own bootlaces he couldn't do both at the same time. Similarly with marching, he could swing his arms and legs together in a close approximation of a soldier on the move but could only manage to do so in a straight line. Thus any order from the drill sergeant to move to the right or the left was ignored by Quinn who simply steamed ahead in a dead straight line.

His progress was normally interrupted by a couple of military policemen who would round him up before he marched into the heavy traffic on the main road and steer him niftily towards the guard house where he spent the greater part of his army career.

Like most sporting nig-nogs he was not lacking in bottle and would have a go at anything. Sadly, his total inability to make any part of his body do what he required of it, plus his determination to become an athlete if it killed him, made him the terror of the gymnasium. To have Quinn in your squad while doing work on apparatus was at once to marvel at the foibles of the human frame when it is out of synchronization, and to wonder at the unquenchable ambition of the sporting nig-nog. Once, required simply to run at the box, leap on it, roll a somersault and jump off at

the other end, Quinn took off and sailed over the box like a bird. He would have undoubtedly gone straight through the wall of the gymnasium like a missile had he not been grabbed in full flight by two startled P T instructors.

In the end they put Quinn in the Education Corps which was the repository for National Service 'weirdos', where he was allowed to wear plimsolls all day long and while away his time dreaming of becoming a sporting hero. He was much attracted to cricket and would spend hours design-ing special equipment to aid the sporting nig-nog in playing the most noble of games. I recall that one invention of his was a large rubber pouch with a special zip fastener attachment to be used by slip fielders.

Quinn was not the only sporting nig-nog of my acquaintance drawn to cricket. In fact, in my experience cricket attracts more SNNs than any other game. Only the other day I watched one performing at my local club. I can spot them a mile off now. In the main they are immediately distinguishable from the rest of their fellow men because they are generally better turned out. One of the characteristics of the sporting nig-nog is that because he can't play as well as his fellow man, he over compensates by having the best gear.

I picked my man immediately. He was at mid-on looking every inch a cricketer except I knew that the first time the ball went near him something outrageous would happen. Sure enough, he managed to convert an innocu-ous push through mid-wicket into four runs by the simple expedient of kicking the ball forty yards to the boundary as he endeavoured to field it. Banished to guard the deep field, he so misjudged a high top-edge that he was some-where near the square leg umpire in pursuit of the catch when the ball went first bounce for four at third man.

His big moment came in the last over of the match when he had to play three balls to save the game for his side. He strode to the wicket looking like a county player. All the gear was expensive and lovingly maintained. As he walked from the pavilion he made a large semi-circular sweep to the stumps thus wasting a bit more time and giving his eyes a better chance to adjust to the late evening sun. He took guard in the grand manner, marking his position with bat and toe, carefully surveying the field, making a mental note of the whereabouts of every player. Then he adjusted his cap, had the sightscreens moved two feet to the left and settled in to save the game for his side.

The first ball he received, a perfectly straightforward delivery, uprooted his off stump with the batsman in the statuesque pose of someone who has just played the ball off his toes through mid-wicket. He would no doubt regale his skipper with stories of how the bowler moved it in from outside leg stump to hit the off, and what a pig of a ball to get first thing. And, no doubt, the skipper would nod in kindly fashion knowing full well that the fellow was simply a hopeless sporting nig-nog.

Unless sporting nig-nogs are treated sympathetically by their more fortunate colleagues they can get into deep trouble. I once played a charity cricket game with an actor who was the sort of sporting nig-nog who couldn't even run without falling down every five yards. We played at The Oval and he was given sole charge of the cover boundary which that day was about 150 yards from the middle.

After the first over the antics of the fielder in pursuing the ball to the boundary and falling down in spectacular fashion every few yards convinced the Surrey players and the large crowd that it would be a laugh to hit as many balls as possible in the direction of this funny fellow who would thus entertain everyone for the greater part of a hot August afternoon.

What few realized was that the so-called comic antics of the actor were in fact the desperate struggles of a sporting nig-nog to do the right thing. Even when he collapsed after chasing a ball to the boundary for the thirtieth consecutive time and was carried from the pitch by the St John Ambulance Brigade men the crowd hooted with glee convinced it was all part of the act.

Suitably revived with slugs of brandy at the interval the actor decided to bat. He was eager to go to the middle and repair his reputation with a fine innings. I knew it couldn't be done, but I offered what I thought was good advice for his survival in the middle. I told him to get on the back foot and have a look at it for a few overs. I advised him to get right back on his stumps with everything in front because he would not be given lbw on a Sunday charity game.

When he walked to the wicket he was greeted with huge hilarity by the spectators certain in the knowledge that they were in for a good laugh. He didn't disappoint them. The first ball bowled at him, a gentle long hop outside leg stump donated by a kindly bowler to make him feel better, was his downfall. Heeding my advice the actor stepped right back, so far back, in fact, that when he swung at the ball to clout it to the square leg boundary he was prevented from doing so by the intervention of three stumps which he mowed to the ground in front of him. It is the only time I have seen a batsman out hit wicket with the stumps a) resembling chopped firewood and b) smashed by the blade of the bat from behind. 'Got too far back,' explained the actor when he came back in the pavilion.

I nodded in sympathy but knew that in spite of his truly horrendous afternoon the actor would a week later still be flitting o'er the greensward in comic pursuit of his unattainable ambitions. For the really nice thing about being a sporting nig-nog is that you never believe you are one.

23 My Old Man

I was never told fairy tales as a child. Instead I heard of Larwood's action and Hobbs's perfection. Before I ever saw him play I knew Len Hutton intimately, and the first time I witnessed Stanley Matthews in the flesh I knew which way he was going even if the full-back didn't. The stories of these gods, and many, many more besides I heard at my father's knee.

He was a remarkable man with a marvellous facility to adorn an anecdote. It was he who invented the gate, complete with attendant, which was built in honour of a Barnsley winger who could run like the wind but didn't know how to stop. At the end of one of his runs down the wing the gate would be open and the winger would career through and out of the ground to finally come to a stop halfway across the car park. Or so Dad said.

It was he who told me of the full-back whose fearsome sliding tackles carried him into the wall surrounding the ground causing the spectators to start wearing goggles at home games for fear of being blinded by flying chips of concrete. Frank Barson, he assured me, once ran the entire length of the field bouncing the ball on his head, beat the opposing goalkeeper and then headed his final effort over the cross bar because he'd had a row with his manager before the game.

Moreover, the old man swore he managed to see Len

Hutton's 364 at The Oval by convincing the gate attendant that he was dying of some incurable disease and his last
wish was to see Len before he took leave of this earth. I
never swallowed that one until once at a football match
where the gates were closed I witnessed him convince a
gateman that he was a journalist and I was his runner. I
was seven at the time, and it was the very first occasion I
watched a football match from a press box.

Apart from being a fairy story teller he was one of the
best all-round sportsmen I have come across. He loved any
game, and as soon as he took it up he played it well. I never
saw him play football, but I have been told that he did a
fair imitation of Wilf Copping. As a cricketer he was a
quick bowler with an action copied from his great hero,
Harold Larwood.

He had a marvellous agility and sure pair of hands near
the bat, and as a batsman he was a genuine No. 11 who
often didn't know whether he'd play left- or right-handed
until he got to the crease. Not that it made much difference.

Of all games he loved cricket the most. He judged
everything and everyone by the game. The only time I ever
saw him lost for words was when someone confessed they
neither knew nor cared about cricket. Then he would shake
his head sadly baffled that a great part of his world – for
cricket was surely that – could mean so little to any other
sane human being. Last season a friend and I took him to
Headingley and sat him behind the bowler's arm and he
never moved all day. We brought him pork pies and
sandwiches and good Yorkshire beer, and he sat under his
native sun watching Lillee bowl fast and he was the
happiest man on our planet.

You always knew where my old man would be on any
cricket ground: right behind the bowler's arm. Moreover,
if ever you lost him, or he lost himself – as he often did being
born without a sense of direction – you simply asked the
whereabouts of the nearest cricket ground and there you

would discover the old man sitting contentedly awaiting the arrival of his search party.

In his younger days his favourite holiday was a week at Scarbro' – which he reckoned had the best beach wicket in Britain – or Butlin's, not because he particularly cared for the idea of a holiday camp, but because of the sporting competitions. He used to enter the lot and normally came home with a couple of trophies for snooker or running or the mixed wheelbarrow race. He entered everything and anything and owed much of his success to his ability to talk an opponent to death. I once heard an irate tennis opponent say to him: 'Doesn't tha' ever shut thi' gob?'

'Only when other people are talking,' said my old man, with a disarming smile.

When he finished playing he took up coaching, first the local youngsters and latterly his three grandchildren. They, like me, are left-handed batsmen. Not because God made them so, but because the old man's theory was that not many players like bowling at left-handers. His other theory, based on a lifetime's experience, was that fast bowlers are crazy, so he determined to make at least one of my sons a slow bowler.

The consequence of this is that I once had the only eight-year-old googly bowler in the Western Hemisphere. At ten he added the top spinner to his repertoire and when he was twelve the old man's face was a picture as his protégé beat me with a googly and then had me plumb in front of the dustbin with one that hurried off the pitch and came straight through.

The old man's name was John William, and he hated John Willy. If anyone addressed him thus when he was playing in his prime, the red alert went up and the casualty ward at Barnsley Beckett Hospital could look forward to receiving visitors.

I have written a lot about him in my many years of writing about cricket, mainly in *The Sunday Times;* indeed the whole basic idea of any cricket article – a mixture of nostalgia and humour – was built on what I had heard at my father's knee.

He's been dead for a couple of cricket seasons now, but I still think about him because he was a special man and I was lucky to know him. He was a Yorkshireman, a miner, a humorist and a fast bowler. Not a bad combination.

I only hope they play cricket in heaven. If they don't he'll ask for a transfer.

24 A Man at Odds

He carries with him the air of a man perpetually at odds with the world. No one suffers the slings and arrows of outrageous fortune – real or imagined – more publicly than Geoff Boycott. When his recall to Test cricket was announced – surely a matter of personal joy – he was heard on television predicting that there would be many people hoping he would fail at Trent Bridge. This somewhat tardy comment surprised no one who has closely observed The World versus Geoffrey Boycott over the past decade or so.

Of all the athletes I know none has worked more assiduously to become the greatest player of his generation, and similarly no one of my acquaintance has paid so little attention to the inevitable consequences of succeeding in that ambition; namely, the business of being a public figure.

Geoffrey Boycott, who neither knows nor cares overmuch about anything else outside of cricket, would claim that his job was to play like the great cricketer he is and not bother about winning any charm contests. Yet there is little doubt – and he knows it, too – that his career in the game would have been a whole lot less turbulent and troublesome had he been able to apply to his life off the field the intelligence and tactical awareness he revealed on it.

Geoffrey Boycott's ruthless drive to succeed has cost him dearly what might be termed his social development. At thirty-six and with fifteen or more years behind him of playing sport at the top-most level, meeting people from all areas of society, travelling the world, he can still be a gauche, uncertain figure. No more, you might say, than many other athletes with the same kind of experience. Which is true, except that Geoffrey Boycott is much more intelligent than the average athlete. He has a keen, sharp mind, he is nobody's fool, and he takes nothing at face value, all of which Mr Kerry Packer will testify to be true. His refusal of Packer's gold was not so much a patriotic gesture; more a careful decision taken after keen perusal of the small print in his contract. Those now locked in combat with Mr Packer and bemoaning the fact that they are unable to obtain a sight of one of these contracts should immediately contact Geoffrey Boycott. He has total recall of what his contained.

The paradox of Geoffrey Boycott is that the man who is absolutely self-sufficient in making such difficult decisions, who has mastered in his own way the intricacies of the most complex of games, is the same person who presents himself as a slightly bitter, embattled figure only at ease in the company of his own beloved Yorkshire team or the handful of people he trusts with complete friendship.

He is, at heart, a loner; more, I suspect, by the circumstances that shaped him rather than by any natural inclination. From the very first moment he played cricket in the Yorkshire mining village where he was born he was determined not simply to play for Yorkshire and England but to be the pre-eminent batsman of his generation. In other words, his ambition was not simply a Yorkshire cap but the laurel wreaths worn by Sutcliffe and Hutton.

Typically, he pursued an alternative career to enter the civil service with the consequent result that throughout his early and late teens, when his contemporaries were indulging in all the possible joys of teenage life, Geoffrey Boycott's existence was divided equally between studying for examinations and practising cricket.

I met him first when he came to play for Barnsley at the age of fifteen. In those days, not fully fleshed out and wearing National Health Service spectacles, he looked an unlikely and puny recruit to a notoriously tough League which took no prisoners. But, from the beginning, he showed himself to be an exceptional talent with an insatiable appetite for learning the game. There was also in this period the first indication of the ruthless streak in his character that later led him into unhappy conflict with some fellow players and the executive.

The story goes that he was playing a friendly Sunday fixture and batting well when play was interrupted to hand him a message asking him to report the next day to Headingley to join the Yorkshire first-team squad. Geoffrey Boycott read the message and walked to the pavilion even though his innings was not finished. He was pursued to the pavilion gate by the opposing skipper who, not unnaturally, pointed out that it was common courtesy to ask his permission before he left the field of play. Moreover, where was he going? Geoffrey Boycott looked at him and said, 'I've finished with this kind of cricket.' And he had.

The answer as to why he chose this course of action – and the answer to a lot of other questions about Geoffrey Boycott – was probably given much later in his career when, as England's opening batsman, he was en route to Australia with Mike Smith's team. Stopping over in Sri Lanka every player in the party had to fill in a form stating, among other things, the purpose of their visit. Everyone completed the form by stating 'cricket'; everyone, that is, except Geoffrey Boycott, who wrote, simply: 'Business'.

It is difficult for anyone, including fellow players, to completely calculate Boycott's total absorption in the game he loves. His idea of relaxation is three-hour net practice, his sole topic of conversation is cricket. He is single, tee-total, non-smoking and still living at home with his mother. In his obsessive dedication to physical fitness, his careful diet, his abhorrence of late nights, he further

isolates himself from the majority of his fellow cricketers who as much enjoy the social side of the game as the playing of it.

He stands out like a Roundhead in a platoon of Cavaliers, and it is this dedication and pride in what he does and what he is that has taken him into the most troubled waters of his turbulent career. Certainly it was the reason for his self-imposed exile from Test cricket. Quite simply Geoffrey Boycott believed that one day he would be captain of England, not because it was his right, but because he was the best man for the job. He swallowed his pride under Denness because he calculated, and correctly, that his days were numbered. It was when Greig was given the vice-captaincy that Boycott foresaw a future whereby he was kept from his ambition not only by a less experienced captain but, moreover, a foreign player. He was deeply hurt by what he considered to be an insulting rejection of his claims. Not for the first time in his life he went his own lonely way.

What changed his mind was Greig's departure and pressure from people around him to display his great talents in the settings they deserve. Anyone who loves the game and delights in watching a great batsman at work can only rejoice at his return and hope that in his years away from Test cricket he has cultivated a more philosophical approach to his relationship with the game. In his darker moments he should remember the boy at Leeds who ran onto the pitch wearing a sweatshirt bearing the legend 'Boycott Bats On Water'. There are more cricket lovers in Britain who would go along with that sentiment than people who would like to see him sink.

If Geoffrey Boycott can loosen just a little the tight rein of his self-discipline and vaunting ambition, we might be lucky enough to see the re-emergence of a great international batsman in the Test arena, and, more importantly, the emergence of a remarkable man with a lot to offer cricket both on and off the field.

There are propitious signs. Recently Yorkshire were playing Nottinghamshire at Trent Bridge and bowling badly. In his eandeavour to stem the flow of runs Boycott was handicapped by injuries to two of his key bowlers. After retrieving the ball from the mid-wicket boundary

Boycott was addressed by a spectator who, in a loud voice, demanded to know why Robinson wasn't given a bowl. Boycott explained that Robinson was injured. Next over, retrieving yet another ball from the same spot, the spectator enquired why Cope wasn't bowling. Again Boycott took time out to explain, patiently and politely, that the bowler was injured. When the same thing happened again a few overs later Boycott told the man that he would speak to him at close of play and explain everything.

Thus at stumps Geoffrey Boycott walked across to the spectator and patiently explained his tactics during the last session of play. After ten minutes of detailed insight into his captaincy and problems he said to the man: 'Now does that satisfy you?'

'All I can say is God help us if they mek thee t'captain of England,' said the spectator.

The point is Geoffrey Boycott told this joke against himself – and laughed out loud at the humour of it all.

25 The Last Word

They have taken down the white fencing in front of the pavilion, and hockey players trample the outfield like a herd of stampeding buffalo. The scoreboard is shuttered and barred like a condemned dwelling, and the alsatian that lives in the house behind the sightscreen will have to wait a few months before it once more indulges its favourite pastime of biting retrieving fielders on the bum.

He will wait a lot more patiently than most of us. Personally, I wish there was a pill to make me sleep through the winter months and awaken on the opening day of the cricket season.

It wasn't always that way. Once upon a time I felt a pang at summer's passing, but soon immersed myself in the joys of a new football season. In those days I used to play a lot, fashioning myself on my great heroes who were always centre-forwards. Centre-forwards, in case anyone has forgotten, were players whose job it was to score goals. On the whole they were large, physically brave men who wore a No. 9 shirt and dedicated themselves to the simple but praiseworthy philosophy that a football's place was in the back of the net, and if it ended up there along with the opposing goalkeeper and centre-half, so much the better.

Today's equivalent, if he exists at all, is called a striker or a target-man. He wears any old number on his shirt to confuse the No. 5 who in any case has a different number

on his back to baffle the No. 9 – if you see what I mean. Don Revie understands and will no doubt one day tell all. In the meantime, the result of this confusion is that lots of players, disguised as someone else, gallop all over the place bumping into other players similarly disguised so that the whole business looks like what it is, a shambles.

Amid all this chaos the striker, or target-man, forgets that his principal job is to score goals, which is why the heroes of my youth are but a pleasant memory of a better day, like Nugget shoe polish and Uncle Joe's mint balls.

Whenever I ran on the field wearing the No. 9 shirt, I was Wally Ardron, or George Robledo, or Cec McCormack, or Tommy Briggs. It mattered little that I could do nothing with my left foot other than stand on it, that I didn't like heading the ball because it mucked my hair for the Saturday night dance. However, I never fancied those defenders, and they were in the majority, who tested the strength of my home-made shin-pads (two folded copies of *Film Fun* down each sock) early in the game. In modern terms, I lacked 'bottle' or 'failed to prove my courage in the tackle'.

However, I let none of these impediments stand in the way of my fantasies, which I developed in the local paper I was reporting for at the time with a series of glowing reports about Ace Goal-grabber Parkinson, or Goal Hungry Mike.

One day a stranger appeared on our touchline and engaged our manager in conversation. After the game I asked the manager who he was.

'Talent scout from Hull City. Came to see thee perform on t'strength of them articles tha's been writin' about thissen,' he said.

'What did he say?' I asked.

'Watched thee for t'first half, then he left saying t'reporter who wrote about thee needed a bloody guide dog,' he said.

I retired shortly after and waited for the cricket by

watching Barnsley. Today there is no such consolation. The football season stretches ahead like a long and dreary road leading to the knacker's yard. It's a journey I'm not willing to take. I think I'll sit at home, like the alsation that lives behind the sightscreen, and wait until I can get my teeth into a new cricket season.